Physical Development and Health

The HighScope Preschool Curriculum

Physical Development and Health

Ann S. Epstein, PhD

HIGHSCOPE PRESS®

Ypsilanti, Michigan

Published by
HighScope® Press

A division of the
HighScope Educational Research Foundation
600 North River Street
Ypsilanti, Michigan 48198-2898
734.485.2000, FAX 734.485.0704
Orders: 800.40.PRESS; Fax: 800.442.4FAX; www.highscope.org
E-mail: *press@highscope.org*

Copyright © 2012 by HighScope Educational Research Foundation. All rights reserved. Except as permitted under the Copyright Act of 1976, no part of this book may be reproduced or distributed in any form or by any means, electronic or mechanical, including photocopy, recording, or any information storage-and-retrieval system, without either the prior written permission from the publisher or authorization through payment of the appropriate per-copy fee to the Copyright Clearance Center, Inc., 222 Rosewood Drive, Danvers, MA 01923, 978.750.8400, fax 978.646.8600, or on the web at www.copyright.com. The name "HighScope" and its corporate logos are registered trademarks and service marks of the HighScope Foundation.

Editor: Nancy Brickman
Cover design, text design: Judy Seling, Seling Design
Production: Judy Seling, Seling Design; Kazuko Sacks, Profit Makers LLC
Photography:
Bob Foran — Front cover, 1, 3, 4 (top left), 8, 22 (left), 23, 24, 28, 29, 35, 36, 47 (top left), 54 (bottom), 56, 61, 65, 68 (top), 74, 77, 86 (bottom), 94 (left), back cover (left)
Gregory Fox — 4 (right), 7, 10, 15, 17, 18–19 (KDI 17, KDI 18, KDI 19, KDI 20), 20, 22 (right), 31, 32, 33, 37 (top left & right, bottom left), 40, 42 (top right, bottom left), 43 (bottom left), 45, 46 (top), 50, 51, 52, 53, 54 (top right), 55, 57, 63, 67, 68 (bottom), 70, 73, 75, 76, 78 (right), 80, 85, 86 (top), 88, 93, 94 (right), back cover (right)
Linda Grimm — 26
HighScope Staff — All other photos

Library of Congress Cataloging-in-Publication Data
Epstein, Ann S.
  Physical development and health / Ann S. Epstein, PhD.
      pages cm. -- (The HighScope preschool curriculum)
  Includes bibliographical references.
  ISBN 978-1-57379-653-8 (soft cover : alk. paper) 1. Physical education for children--Study and teaching (Preschool) 2. Physical education for children--Curricula. I. Title.
  GV443.E67 2012
  372.86--dc23
                                        2012003700

Printed in the United States of America
10 9 8 7 6 5 4 3

Contents

Acknowledgments vii

Chapter 1. The Importance of Physical Development and Health 1
What Is Physical Development and Health? 2
Physical Development and Learning: Not Automatic 2
The Multiple Benefits of Movement and Health Education 5
Developmental Stages and Principles of Physical Development 9
About This Book 11

Chapter 2. General Teaching Strategies for Physical Development and Health 15
General Teaching Strategies 16
    Provide space for children to explore and practice motor skills 16
    Provide children with equipment and materials for exploring and practicing motor and self-help skills 21
    Provide time for children to explore and practice motor and self-help skills throughout the day 23
    Model and guide emerging physical skills and healthy behaviors 24
    Add language to describe behavior related to physical development and health 27
Key Developmental Indicators in Physical Development and Health 29

Chapter 3. KDI 16. Gross-Motor Skills 31
How Gross-Motor Skills Develop 32
Teaching Strategies That Support Gross-Motor Skills 36
    Encourage children to explore a wide range of positions and movements 36
    Encourage children to build movement skills in sequence 38
    Provide interesting materials to accompany children's movements 41
    Provide children with experiences and materials for exploring movement concepts 44
Ideas for Scaffolding KDI 16. Gross-Motor Skills 48

Chapter 4. KDI 17. Fine-Motor Skills 49
How Fine-Motor Skills Develop 50
Teaching Strategies That Support Fine-Motor Skills 52
    Provide materials and activities that require the use of fingers and hands 52
    Provide similar objects in a range of sizes and shapes that children can handle 57
Ideas for Scaffolding KDI 17. Fine-Motor Skills 58

Chapter 5. KDI 18. Body Awareness 61
How Body Awareness Develops 63
Teaching Strategies That Support Body Awareness 64
    Create environments and activities that allow children to explore personal (self) space and general (shared) space 64
    Provide opportunities for children to move through different types of space in different ways 65
    Provide opportunities for children to feel and move their bodies to a steady beat 67
    Help children learn the names and functions of body parts 69
Ideas for Scaffolding KDI 18. Body Awareness 71

Chapter 6. KDI 19. Personal Care 73

   How Personal Care Develops 74

   Teaching Strategies That Support Personal Care 76

      Let children do things for themselves 76

      Provide children with activities and equipment for practicing the skills needed for personal care routines 78

   Ideas for Scaffolding KDI 19. Personal Care 81

Chapter 7. KDI 20. Healthy Behavior 83

   How Healthy Behavior Develops 84

   Teaching Strategies That Support Healthy Behavior 89

      Model healthy behavior yourself 89

      Provide opportunities for children to engage in healthy behavior 89

   Ideas for Scaffolding KDI 20. Healthy Behavior 92

References 95

Acknowledgments

Many people contributed their knowledge and skills to the publication of *Physical Development and Health*. I want to thank the early childhood and other staff members who collaborated on creating the key developmental indicators (KDIs) in this content area: Beth Marshall, Sue Gainsley, Shannon Lockhart, Polly Neill, Kay Rush, Julie Hoelscher, Emily Thompson, and Karen Sawyers. Among this group of colleagues, those who devoted special attention to reviewing the manuscript for this book were Shannon Lockhart, Kay Rush, and Karen Sawyers. Karen Sawyers also assisted with photo selection. Mary Hohmann, whose expertise informs many other HighScope curriculum books, also provided detailed feedback.

The developmental scaffolding charts in this volume — describing what children might do and say and how adults can support and gently extend their learning at different developmental levels — are invaluable contributions to the curriculum. I am grateful to Beth Marshall and Sue Gainsley for the extraordinary working relationship we forged in creating these charts. By bringing our unique experiences to this challenging process, we integrated knowledge about child development and effective classroom practices from the perspectives of research, teaching, training, and policy.

Thanks are also due to Nancy Brickman, who edited this volume, and Katie Bruckner, who assisted with all aspects of the publication process. I also want to acknowledge the following individuals for contributing to the book's visual appeal and reader friendliness: photographers Bob Foran and Gregory Fox, and graphic artists Judy Seling (book designer) and Kazuko Sacks (book production).

Finally, I extend sincerest thanks to all the teachers, trainers, children, and families whose participation in HighScope and other early childhood programs has contributed to the creation and authenticity of the HighScope Preschool Curriculum over the decades. I hope this book continues to support their learning in physical development and health for many years to come.

CHAPTER *1*

The Importance of Physical Development and Health

What Is Physical Development and Health?

Young children enjoy practicing the physical challenges they set for themselves — over and over again. You can see their satisfaction as they learn how to bend and twist, run and hop, throw and catch. The concentration on their faces is evident as they poke and squeeze play dough, explore various writing tools, tear and cut paper, string beads, pour juice, and pound nails.

Learning in physical development and health is a concrete experience for young children, not an abstract lesson in bodily care (see examples, right). Gretchen expends real energy riding that scooter, and Oliver is intent when he strings beads. Likewise, Rowan learns about herself by looking in the mirror and at the bodies of others. Children like Miriam and Seth are proud when they can tend to their own needs. For Lynette, food becomes a meaningful topic of conversation when a meal is shared with friends.

Physical Development and Learning: Not Automatic

The idea that children need to be taught to develop physically may seem odd. We assume such growth happens naturally, provided children receive adequate nutrition and have opportunities to use their large and small muscles in a safe environment. Since children seek out physical challenges without adult prodding, why should educators include physical development in an early childhood curriculum?

Although healthy bodies grow and develop on their own, it is nevertheless important for early childhood programs to provide appropriate physical activities and nutritious meals and snacks for young children. As infants and toddlers, children master the basics of getting

Physical Development and Health in Action

At outside time, Gretchen pushes with one leg on the ground while balancing the other leg on the scooter. Then she puts her whole body on the scooter and rides it between the shed and the ramp.

❖

At small-group time, Oliver shows his teacher Val how he can put beads on a string. "My sister showed me how to do it and I remembered," he says with pride.

❖

At recall time, Rowan says, "Foreheads hold up your eyebrows."

❖

At greeting time, Miriam covers her mouth to "catch her cough" in her elbow. She does the same thing later at small-group time.

❖

At outside time, Seth bends down and ties his own shoes. He takes a few minutes to admire his accomplishment before returning to the sandbox.

❖

At snacktime, Lynette explains to her teacher the four steps she will use to make a sandwich: set out two pieces of bread, spread peanut butter on one and honey on the other, then put the pieces together. "My mommy says honey is more healthy than jelly," she says.

around and handling materials. The preschool years then open the door to refining those basic skills and expanding gross- and fine-motor capabilities. Therefore, young children need daily vigorous exercise that is fun and interesting. They also benefit physically, mentally, and socially from a relaxed social environment where they can eat healthy foods with a variety of pleasing tastes and textures.

Of course, there is a natural biological progression of gross- and fine-motor development in the early years (see Copple & Bredekamp, 2009). Major advances in physical development are obvious in infancy and toddlerhood, as children progress through the milestones of holding their heads up, turning over, creeping, crawling, and walking. Children also make significant gains during preschool. Their large muscles grow in size and strength and they gain increasing control over the movements, balance, and coordination of their bodies. Fine-motor skills improve as young children increase their hand-eye coordination, the strength and flexibility of their grasp, and their ability to control and manipulate objects.

> "By accepting the unity of mind and body, we come one step closer to genuine developmental appropriateness. After all, if we are to truly educate the whole child, we must first recognize children as thinking, feeling, moving human beings."
>
> — Pica (1997, p. 4)

To develop the full range of physical skills, children need the support of adults who introduce appropriate materials, plan experiences, and scaffold learning in the moment.

4 *Physical Development and Health*

Children eagerly tackle physical challenges as they pursue their aims and interests. It takes concentration and coordination to "fish" for the tin lid you want, balance on a block structure you helped to create, or use hands, chest, and chin to hold on to as many apples as possible.

At the same time that children learn about what their bodies can do, they also become increasingly aware of how to take care of them. Preschoolers take pride in mastering self-help skills. They learn that being physically active is not only fun, but good for their bodies. With adult guidance, young children also begin to understand how proper nutrition helps them grow up to be strong and healthy.

However, it is a mistake to view these changes as purely maturational. Many factors at home, in school, and in the culture at large affect children's physical development. Research confirms that young children do not learn basic physical skills simply through unguided play (Manross, 2000). For example, left on their own to respond to music, preschoolers tend not to use all their movement capabilities (Stellaccio & McCarthy, 1999). Three-year-olds are more likely to remain stationary (swaying, bending, moving their arms and heads), while four- to five-year-olds tend to move around (sliding, hopping, running). Whether they remain in place or are mobile, young children also tend to limit their movements to repeating a few patterns.

To help children develop all their physical capacities, adults must explicitly plan activities that exercise their large and small muscles. They must also provide children with time, space, and equipment to practice those skills. Professor Stephen Sanders, a pioneer in the development of preschool movement curricula, says, "Play provides children with the opportunity to practice movement skills in a variety of contexts. [However,] some structuring of physical activity is necessary to help children maximize their movement experiences" (2002, p. 31). For example, note how the teacher in this scenario helps children extend learning that originally arose from a child's observations about how he moved:

During a game of galloping, Bryant tells Beth that he is going to be a "crooked horse." When Beth asks what he means, Bryant begins to gallop in a zigzag path. "See," he says, "I went crooked." "You galloped in a crooked path to the tree," Beth agrees. "I'm going to gallop in a crooked path too," she says. And she does so, adding, "Sometimes I call this 'going zigzag.'" "Yeah, like Rags," Bryant says, referring to a dog who "goes zigzag" in a favorite class song. Several other children also imitate this movement. After a few days of crooked-path galloping, Beth says to the group, "I wonder what other kinds of paths we could gallop in." Corrin suggests "circles," and they all gallop in a series of curves. Other ideas follow: sideways, forward and back, "baby [small] gallops," and "monster [big] gallops."

Moreover, the acquisition of healthy habits is by no means automatic either. In fact, current concerns about childhood obesity and children's lack of physical activity make educators and policymakers more aware than ever of the need to make physical development and health a standard part of the early childhood curriculum. Children's minds as well as their bodies will benefit from educators' conscious and conscientious attention to this content area.

The Multiple Benefits of Movement and Health Education

Movement education has received increasing national attention because of its potential health benefits. This country has seen an unprecedented rise in obesity in children, which puts them at risk for diabetes, heart disease, high blood pressure, colon cancer and other health problems in adulthood. The percentage of

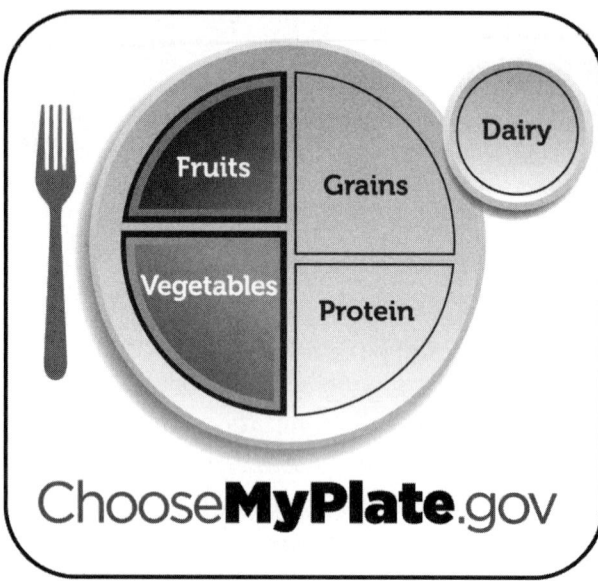

The federal government's Choose My Plate campaign, which provides materials for helping young children learn about nutrition, reflects the increased attention now being focused on preventing childhood obesity.

children identified as overweight has more than doubled in the past 30 years. According to the White House Task Force on Childhood Obesity (2010), one in five children is overweight or obese by the time they reach their sixth birthday; over half of obese children are overweight at or before the age of two. The preschool years are crucial to prevent the development of obesity, since fat tissue is laid down primarily between the ages of three and seven. If children have a high body-mass index (BMI) between four and six years of age, they are significantly more likely to be obese as adults.

Along with poor diet, "physical inactivity has contributed to the 100% increase in the prevalence of childhood obesity in the United States since 1980" (Sanders, 2002, p. xiii). By contrast, children who develop basic motor skills and are physically active are more likely to become healthy adults (National Center for Health Statistics, 2004). The media play a large role in the early onset of obesity, both by contributing to inactivity and by advertising unhealthy foods. Although the American Academy of Pediatrics (AAP) Committee on Public Education (2001) recommends that children under age two watch no television and children over age two watch no more than one to two hours a day of quality media, research shows that 43 percent of children under age two watch television daily, and 90 percent of children aged four to six use screen media an average of two hours per day. Studies cited by AAP show a significant correlation between watching media and being overweight. The guidelines issued by the National Association for Sport and Physical Education (NASPE, 2009) recommend that preschoolers get *at least* one hour a day of vigorous physical activity, yet studies of time spent at home and in early childhood settings show most children fall far short of this goal.[1]

In addition to promoting good health, developing physical abilities is also important in its own right. As stated in the Nebraska Department of Education Early Learning Guidelines (2005), "physical development and health and safety activities should be integrated into all areas of learning. Activities should be structured to encourage preschool children to explore their world, promote coordination and strength, enhance thinking skills, and develop an 'I can do it' attitude. The development of fine-motor and gross-motor skills, as well as of self-help skills, is a critical part of the development of the preschool child. These skills serve as the foundation for the development of future academic skills such as writing and reading" (p. 31).

---

[1]The one-hour per day recommendation for vigorous physical activity refers to the entire day, that is, time spent both in and out of preschool. It does not mean that programs themselves need to schedule an hour a day for such activity but that they should contribute to it.

Physical Activity Guidelines for Preschoolers

"**Guideline 1.** Preschoolers should accumulate at least 60 minutes of structured physical activity each day.

Guideline 2. Preschoolers should engage in at least 60 minutes — and up to several hours — of unstructured physical activity each day, and should not be sedentary for more than 60 minutes at a time, except when sleeping.

Guideline 3. Preschoolers should be encouraged to develop competence in fundamental motor skills that will serve as the building blocks for future motor skillfulness and physical activity.

Guideline 4. Preschoolers should have access to indoor and outdoor areas that meet or exceed recommended safety standards for performing large-muscle activities.

Guideline 5. Caregivers and parents in charge of preschoolers' health and well-being are responsible for understanding the importance of physical activity and for promoting movement skills by providing opportunities for structured and unstructured physical activity."

— National Association for Sport and Physical Education (2009, p. 24)

Reprinted from *Active Start: A Statement of Physical Activity Guidelines for Children From Birth to Five Years,* with permission from the National Association for Sport and Physical Education (NASPE), 1900 Association Drive, Reston, VA 20191. www.naspeinfo.org.

Everyday tasks often require balance, coordination, and other physical skills. Helping out at snack- and mealtimes allows children to practice these motor skills and fosters an "I can do it" attitude.

Developing and exercising gross- and fine-motor skills serves multiple functions. Balance and coordination are essential to accomplishing many everyday tasks. Movement and manipulation are also inherently pleasurable. Children enjoy moving their bodies, whether they are simply feeling the freedom of exercising their muscles or expressing creativity. Likewise, they

Physical skills develop in tandem with abilities in other areas. In this activity, children develop body awareness, balance, social skills, and spatial concepts as they maneuver around classmates on a path of tree-stump slices.

find satisfaction in handling objects to achieve a goal, be it stacking blocks or painting a picture.

Physical development also promotes learning in literacy, mathematics, science, and social-emotional areas. For example, acting out stories aids children's narrative comprehension. Writing requires manual coordination and dexterity. Moving helps children develop spatial concepts, which are a component of geometry. Counting repeated movements (steps, hops, pats) enhances early number awareness. When children describe and compare speeds, directions, and changes in motion (their own and others'), they are beginning to lay the groundwork for understanding the physics of motion. Respecting personal space, knowing when and how to touch others, or collaborating on physical challenges, such as building a large structure, are all aspects of developing social relationships.

Rae Pica (1997), a children's movement specialist, makes no distinction between physical and academic learning. "In many early childhood programs, teachers are torn between what they know about how young children learn and preparing children for 'academic' learning. But the truth is, not only does movement stimulate learning physiologically, but it also helps young children to experience concepts so they can process them cognitively. Teachers must offer children opportunities to solve movement problems, invent their own solutions to challenges, and make abstract concepts (like high and low) concrete by physically experiencing them. [Action] is the key to learning for the young child" (p. 4).

In fact, research shows how the development of children's minds and bodies are inextricably connected. Brain researcher Eric Jensen (2000) emphasizes that the mere act of moving increases heart rate and circulation, thereby sending more oxygen to key areas of the brain. The relationship between physical and social abilities also has implications for learning. Children who are physically competent are seen more positively by peers and adults and therefore have better relationships with others. They can then use social interactions as a venue for learning. Physically adept children are also more willing to tackle intellectual challenges, and feel confident about their ability to master new skills and knowledge. As a result, they do better in school than children who are physically insecure or awkward (Gallahue & Donnelly, 2003).

Stephen Sanders makes similar comments about the connections between physical and social skills: "It is important that teachers do everything possible not to turn children off to physical activity or promote negative feelings of self-worth....The type of activities children experience in the learning environment influences how they interact socially with each other not only in movement class but long after they return to their classroom and as they play and interact at home with friends, peers, and family" (2002, p. 29).

Developmental Stages and Principles of Physical Development

As children hone their gross- and fine-motor physical abilities, they generally progress through the following four developmental stages or levels of proficiency (Graham, Holt/Hale, & Parker, 2004). There is great individual variability, but preschoolers are typically at the first two levels.

Precontrol level (beginner). Children at this level cannot consciously control or intentionally replicate a movement except under limited conditions (turning toward a familiar voice, sipping from a cup like older family members, making a beeline for the door when Mommy or Daddy comes home). As their bodies stretch after toddlerhood (especially in the legs and trunk), their perception of their own size often lags behind their actual size (Wood, 2007). Children's actions often lack coordination and fluidity, and they need many opportunities for exploration and sensory feedback to discover what their bodies can do.

Control level (advanced beginner). Children's movements are less haphazard as their bodies begin to respond more fluidly to their intentions. They still require ample time to explore and practice. To learn a new physical skill, children need to experience success at least 80 percent of the time (Sanders, 2002).

Utilization level (intermediate). Children are capable of an increasing range of automatic movements. For example, they no longer pause to "think" before engaging in more complex actions like bouncing a ball or climbing up a jungle gym. Children are capable of joining one movement skill with another in a simple game-like situation.

Proficiency level (advanced). Children's basic movements become more automatic and begin to seem effortless. They are able to refine specific skills and their level of physical competence becomes increasingly advanced. Children are now ready to participate in formal games.

In addition to these stages, there are also two general principles that apply to early motor development, with implications for classroom practices. The first is that *the development of motor skills is sequential*. According to David L. Gallahue, "No matter what the activity, one cannot take part successfully if the essential fundamental movement skills contained within that activity have not been mastered" (1995, p. 126). Consequently, physical education programs no longer focus on discrete "units" such as three weeks of throwing followed by three weeks of skipping, but provide a variety of motor experiences throughout the year for practice and cumulative mastery. Like other content areas, physical experiences for young children should be designed so that later learning builds on earlier knowledge and skills.

The second principle is that *preschool movement programs and youth sports are different* (Pica, 2004). Formal sports are only appropriate

10   Physical Development and Health

Motor skills develop in predictable sequences. The child at right still needs to use both hands to hold a hammer while the child at left has learned to control a hammer with one hand.

for older children who have the specific skills needed to compete. Most children do not attain this readiness until age six or seven, and for many it is even later. By contrast, movement programs for young children emphasize self-improvement, involvement, and cooperation, instead of competition. "Physical activity has a powerful influence on how children feel about themselves," says Sanders (2002, p. 29). Therefore, every child who wants to should be encouraged to participate. Elimination activities exclude children and leave a large group of inactive, restless youngsters. With this principle in mind, early physical education programs should focus on building basic skills, not on games and sports with winners and losers. For example, when playing musical chairs, there should be enough chairs for everyone (even extra chairs) in every round. This way, the focus is on everyone finding a chair when the music stops or the leader says the "magic word," never on eliminating players until one is left.

In including physical development and health as a component of school readiness, the National Education Goals Panel (Kagan, Moore, & Bredekamp, 1995) cites extensive research linking health to academic performance. Factors such as prenatal care and early nutrition affect brain development, which in turn impacts virtually every area of physical, mental, and social development. Maintaining good health and developing physical skills have many benefits for young children. As stated earlier, using their bodies to accomplish physical feats and complete challenging tasks is gratifying to them. Physical development is also a way for children to learn other cognitive and social concepts, such as ideas about space and forming human relationships. When we help children develop physically, we endow them with a valuable self-image and a pathway to learning.

About This Book

In the HighScope Preschool Curriculum, the content of children's learning is organized into eight areas: A. Approaches to Learning; B. Social and Emotional Development; C. Physical Development and Health; D. Language, Literacy, and Communication; E. Mathematics; F. Creative Arts; G. Science and Technology; and H. Social Studies. Within each content area, HighScope identifies **key developmental indicators (KDIs)** that are the building blocks of young children's thinking and reasoning. (See the next two pages for a chart showing the 58 preschool KDIs.)

The term *key developmental indicators* encapsulates HighScope's approach to early education. The word *key* refers to the fact that these are the meaningful ideas children should learn and experience. The second part of the term — *developmental* — conveys the idea that learning is gradual and cumulative. Learning follows a sequence, generally moving from simple to more complex knowledge and skills. Finally, we chose the term *indicators* to emphasize that educators need evidence that children are developing the knowledge, skills, and understanding considered important for school and life readiness. To plan appropriately for students and to evaluate program effectiveness, we need observable indicators of our impact on children.

This book is designed as a guide to help you understand and scaffold (support and gently extend) young children's learning in HighScope's Physical Development and Health content area. This chapter discussed why the skills and abilities in this content area are so important for young children in today's world. It provided insights from the research literature on the sequences of physical development and basic principles for supporting children as they acquire physical abilities, healthy practices, and knowledge about how their bodies work.

Chapter 2 describes general teaching strategies for developing physical skills and healthy behaviors. Chapters 3–7, respectively, provide specific teaching strategies for each of the five KDIs in this curriculum content area:

16. **Gross-motor skills:** Children demonstrate strength, flexibility, balance, and timing in using their large muscles.

17. **Fine-motor skills:** Children demonstrate dexterity and hand-eye coordination in using their small muscles.

18. **Body awareness:** Children know about their bodies and how to navigate them in space.

19. **Personal care:** Children carry out personal care routines on their own.

20. **Healthy behavior:** Children engage in healthy practices.

At the end of each of these chapters is a chart showing ideas for scaffolding learning for that KDI. The chart will help you recognize the specific abilities that are developing at earlier, middle, and later stages of development and gives corresponding teaching strategies you can use to support and gently extend children's learning at each stage.

HighScope Preschool Curriculum Content
Key Developmental Indicators

A. Approaches to Learning

1. **Initiative:** Children demonstrate initiative as they explore their world.
2. **Planning:** Children make plans and follow through on their intentions.
3. **Engagement:** Children focus on activities that interest them.
4. **Problem solving:** Children solve problems encountered in play.
5. **Use of resources:** Children gather information and formulate ideas about their world.
6. **Reflection:** Children reflect on their experiences.

B. Social and Emotional Development

7. **Self-identity:** Children have a positive self-identity.
8. **Sense of competence:** Children feel they are competent.
9. **Emotions:** Children recognize, label, and regulate their feelings.
10. **Empathy:** Children demonstrate empathy toward others.
11. **Community:** Children participate in the community of the classroom.
12. **Building relationships:** Children build relationships with other children and adults.
13. **Cooperative play:** Children engage in cooperative play.
14. **Moral development:** Children develop an internal sense of right and wrong.
15. **Conflict resolution:** Children resolve social conflicts.

C. Physical Development and Health

16. **Gross-motor skills:** Children demonstrate strength, flexibility, balance, and timing in using their large muscles.
17. **Fine-motor skills:** Children demonstrate dexterity and hand-eye coordination in using their small muscles.
18. **Body awareness:** Children know about their bodies and how to navigate them in space.
19. **Personal care:** Children carry out personal care routines on their own.
20. **Healthy behavior:** Children engage in healthy practices.

D. Language, Literacy, and Communication[2]

21. **Comprehension:** Children understand language.
22. **Speaking:** Children express themselves using language.
23. **Vocabulary:** Children understand and use a variety of words and phrases.
24. **Phonological awareness:** Children identify distinct sounds in spoken language.
25. **Alphabetic knowledge:** Children identify letter names and their sounds.
26. **Reading:** Children read for pleasure and information.
27. **Concepts about print:** Children demonstrate knowledge about environmental print.
28. **Book knowledge:** Children demonstrate knowledge about books.
29. **Writing:** Children write for many different purposes.
30. **English language learning:** (If applicable) Children use English and their home language(s) (including sign language).

---

[2] KDIs 21–29 may be used for the child's home language(s) as well as English. KDI 30 refers specifically to English language learning.

E. Mathematics

31. **Number words and symbols**: Children recognize and use number words and symbols.
32. **Counting**: Children count things.
33. **Part-whole relationships**: Children combine and separate quantities of objects.
34. **Shapes**: Children identify, name, and describe shapes.
35. **Spatial awareness**: Children recognize spatial relationships among people and objects.
36. **Measuring**: Children measure to describe, compare, and order things.
37. **Unit**: Children understand and use the concept of unit.
38. **Patterns**: Children identify, describe, copy, complete, and create patterns.
39. **Data analysis**: Children use information about quantity to draw conclusions, make decisions, and solve problems.

F. Creative Arts

40. **Art**: Children express and represent what they observe, think, imagine, and feel through two- and three-dimensional art.
41. **Music**: Children express and represent what they observe, think, imagine, and feel through music.
42. **Movement**: Children express and represent what they observe, think, imagine, and feel through movement.
43. **Pretend play**: Children express and represent what they observe, think, imagine, and feel through pretend play.
44. **Appreciating the arts**: Children appreciate the creative arts.

G. Science and Technology

45. **Observing**: Children observe the materials and processes in their environment.
46. **Classifying**: Children classify materials, actions, people, and events.
47. **Experimenting**: Children experiment to test their ideas.
48. **Predicting**: Children predict what they expect will happen.
49. **Drawing conclusions**: Children draw conclusions based on their experiences and observations.
50. **Communicating ideas**: Children communicate their ideas about the characteristics of things and how they work.
51. **Natural and physical world**: Children gather knowledge about the natural and physical world.
52. **Tools and technology**: Children explore and use tools and technology.

H. Social Studies

53. **Diversity**: Children understand that people have diverse characteristics, interests, and abilities.
54. **Community roles**: Children recognize that people have different roles and functions in the community.
55. **Decision making**: Children participate in making classroom decisions.
56. **Geography**: Children recognize and interpret features and locations in their environment.
57. **History**: Children understand past, present, and future.
58. **Ecology**: Children understand the importance of taking care of their environment.

CHAPTER 2

General Teaching Strategies for Physical Development and Health

Adults design and equip their indoor and outdoor spaces and plan a variety of physical activities to contribute to children's gross- and fine-motor development. They acknowledge that preschoolers are interested in and increasingly capable of taking care of their own bodily needs by providing opportunities for and encouraging self-help skills. In addition, they ensure that young children's health, safety, and nutritional needs are met in the program environment. The following are general suggestions that can be used by teachers to support children as they develop a wide range of physical skills and healthy practices.

General Teaching Strategies

To promote preschoolers' physical development and health, use the general strategies that follow.

Provide space for children to explore and practice motor skills

To develop gross-motor skills, young children need large open spaces where they can move their bodies freely without bumping into objects or one another. Note how open space contributes to these learning experiences:

At outside time, Maeve runs around the climber.

At outside time, Anna and Jessa walk all the way around the playground "looking for bugs to put in bug catchers."

At work time in the block area, Christopher and Athi jump from block to block. "Don't step in the water," Christopher warns, "or the alligators will get you!" "They'll bite your foot off," adds Athi. Ruth, their teacher, asks if the alligators will bite her. "Yeah," says Christopher and tells her to get on a block. When Ruth is safely on a block, Christopher continues, "Now, when I tell you, jump!" Ruth jumps up and lands on the block where she is standing. "Like this?" she asks. "No, you've got to jump over there to that other block," says Christopher. "Oh, like this," says Ruth. "Yeah. Now you're safe," replies Christopher.

Classrooms should have unobstructed spaces, like the spacious block area on the next page, to make room for movement activities at large-group time as well as for constructions and other projects at work time. If classroom space is limited, teachers may need to plan flexible uses of certain areas; for example, the same open space can be the block area at work time and the usual location for large-group time. Depending on the size of the program's facilities, equipment and materials may need to be moved aside to make space for children's movements. Here are some useful movable storage items that are helpful for programs in which space is used for multiple functions or shared by another program:

- Casters or wheels on interest area storage shelves that make them easy to turn and move against the wall for storage
- Hinged storage shelves that close up like boxes
- Storage tubs that fit under beds, sofas, and easy chairs
- Storage tubs or boxes that stack behind couches or in closets, hallways, and entryways
- Toy baskets and containers stored on wheeled carts

General Teaching Strategies for Physical Development and Health 17

To exercise their large muscles, children need ample open spaces both indoors and outside.

18 *Physical Development and Health*

Physical Development and Health in Action

KDI 16. Gross-motor skills

KDI 17. Fine-motor skills

KDI 18. Body awareness

General Teaching Strategies for Physical Development and Health 19

KDI 19. Personal care

KDI 20. Healthy behavior

Physical Development and Health

Child-height work surfaces sheltered from foot traffic and noise allow children to practice fine-motor skills comfortably and without distractions.

In addition to open classroom spaces, children need the freedom to move outdoors, either in an on-site play yard or nearby playground. If weather and/or safety conditions make this difficult, a gym or multipurpose room can serve as a substitute, but whenever and wherever possible, outdoor spaces are preferable.

Young children also need quiet and protected spaces to practice fine-motor skills without visual and auditory distractions. Uncluttered tables at child height provide flat surfaces for working with small toys, writing tools, art materials, and so on. Preschoolers can also work comfortably on the floor, at easels, on paper tacked to the wall, on outdoor pavement, at sand and water tables, in flower gardens and digging areas, and many other such spaces where they can use their small muscles and hone their hand-eye coordination with a variety of interesting materials and tools:

At work time in the toy area, Maxwell sits at the table, stringing red and green beads. "I'm making a tool belt for Binny [his afternoon day care provider]," he tells his teacher.

❖

At small-group time, the teacher unrolls a sheet of butcher paper on the floor and the children make a class collage with the items they collected the day before on their walk to the beach. Using glue and tape, they attach the shells, pebbles, seaweed, and twigs they sorted. Dottie draws a squiggly line along the bottom of the paper. "Like the waves," she tells her teacher.

❖

At work time in the house area, Penny writes numbers on a memo pad. "This is the bill for the restaurant," she tells Brian, a visiting parent. "I have to write them small so they'll all fit."

❖

At outside time, Simon pokes a row of holes in the flower garden, leaving "lots of space" (about six inches) between them. "If they're too close, the stems get tangled," he explains to his friend Ferris. "My grandma told me. I help her plant her garden."

Wherever physical learning takes place, safety is a primary concern. Environments should be free of obstacles and hazards that can cause children to trip, skid, bump into sharp surfaces, or hurt themselves in other ways. The early childhood program manual *Healthy Young Children* (Aronson, 2002) offers detailed recommendations that include the following general guidelines:

- Allow enough space around furniture and equipment for traffic to flow around them.
- Bolt top-heavy furniture to the wall or floor.
- Place movable furniture away from windows, cabinets, and shelves to prevent climbing hazards.
- Break up long aisles to discourage running.
- For all indoor and outdoor equipment, check the product information and safety standards issued by the Consumer Product Safety Commission (CPSC; www.cpsc.gov).

Provide children with equipment and materials for exploring and practicing motor and self-help skills

Child-friendly equipment and materials are essential to support and encourage children's natural desire to explore their physical abilities. According to Stephen Sanders, "Learning to move is like learning to read, write, or understand principles of math and science in that each requires a manipulative of some type to best develop skills and knowledge in a content area" (2002, p. 25). For example, consider how the materials and equipment that are available in these illustrations lead to specific kinds of movement or self-help experiences:

At outside time, Corrin climbs hands-first to the middle of the inverted U-shaped climber, stops in the middle, turns around, and climbs feet-first down the other side.

❖

At outside time, Tasha asks Sue, her teacher, to play catch with the small bouncy ball. Tasha takes turns bouncing the ball back and forth with Sue.

❖

At large-group time, Malia and Sean attach colorful streamers around their wrists with elastic bands and watch them flutter as they run. "Look, our arms are flying," they say.

❖

Provide multiple wheeled toys and other popular items, as well as easy-to-find alternatives, so children don't have long waits to use materials.

Materials that can be easily set in motion like scarves (above) and beanbags can be used in a variety of movement experiences.

After snacktime, Rolf takes the toothbrush from the holder labeled with his letter link and brushes his teeth. "Up, down, up, down," his teacher chants with each stroke. Rolf turns the water on and off several times to watch it swirl down the drain.

Materials for physical learning should be varied and plentiful so children have choices and do not have to wait for long periods to use a material. It is not necessary or realistic for programs to have one of everything for each child, but children should be able to use many of the items together or in rotation, and also to easily find alternatives for carrying out their large- and small-scale movement intentions.

Developing gross-motor skills in preschool requires equipment for climbing, riding, sliding, and balancing as well as objects children can manipulate such as balls, beanbags, scarves, hoops, and ropes. Young children's fine-motor skills are honed when they use art materials, writing tools, dress-up clothes, household utensils, blocks and other construction toys and tools, puzzles, stacking and nesting toys, beads, and items that can be taken apart and put back together. Some items are only available commercially, such as a sturdy set of wooden blocks, but are well worth the investment. Others can be made or collected at minimal cost, especially with contributions from children's families and local businesses.

Provide time for children to explore and practice motor and self-help skills throughout the day

Teachers often associate particular times of day with particular kinds of movement skills or healthy practices. For example, gross-motor movement activities often happen during large-group time and outside time, and learning about healthy foods frequently occurs during snacks and meals. However, other regularly scheduled activities such as greeting time, message board, work time, small-group time, cleanup time, and transitions also provide opportunities for preschoolers to exercise large and small muscles, learn about their bodies, practice taking care of their physical needs, and engage in health-promoting practices. Consider these examples:

*At **message board**, Amari is excited because his mother and baby sister will be visiting at snacktime. He draws a large and small figure on the message board to represent them.*

*At **small-group time**, the children count the number of beanbags they toss into a big basket.*

*At **work time**, Saul turns the pages of a book and points to the picture of the dog each time it appears. Julian does puzzles. Lila paints with sponges at the easel. Matthew strings beads. Karl digs at the sand table. Maria uses a hammer to bang golf tees into a block of Styrofoam.*

*At **cleanup time**, Felix "skates" from the house area to the block area as he returns small blocks to the shelf. As he stacks the blocks, he lines up their corners precisely.*

We expect to see gross-motor movement (right) at outside time, but it's also a time to exercise the small muscles (left). Both kinds of movement require well-planned spaces and appropriate materials.

*At **recall time**, Yolanda demonstrates how she washed and dressed the baby dolls. Quentin shows the group how he stirred the "bear soup" and ladled it into bowls.*

*At **planning time**, the teacher and children make a "train" with their bodies and move around the work areas. As children find a material they want to work with, they "jump" off the train.*

*At the **transition to snacktime**, the children pretend they are monsters. Jason takes "huge steps." Carly moves with "giant jumps." Shirelle holds her arms out in front of her and curls her hands into claws. Hal says he is a "spinning monster" and twirls his way to the table.*

❖

At planning time, to indicate where they will play, children toss beanbags into buckets marked with each play area's symbol and name. This allows children to practice targeted throwing with an object that is easy for them to handle and control.

*At **snacktime**, Ibrahim pours his own juice and holds Mara's cup steady while she pours hers. He wets a towel to wipe his place when he is done eating and throws it in the trash.*

❖

*At **large-group time**, children take turns being the leader and move their bodies around the circle in different ways, for example, walking forward and backward, sliding sideways, jumping, and skating.*

❖

*At **outside time**, Nate practices opening and closing the Velcro attachment on his sneakers. Gina and Aaron ride the "rocket bus" while Sasha and Ben pull them. They decide it's easier to move on the pavement than on the grass. Isaac rolls down the hill with his arms held tight against his sides. Kevin and Delia chase each other back and forth between two oak trees.*

Model and guide emerging physical skills and healthy behaviors

Although preschoolers' physical abilities have come a long way since toddlerhood, remember that they are constantly learning and their bodies are still changing. Likewise their capacity to take care of their own needs and adopt healthy behaviors continues to evolve during this period. To effectively support children's early learning in physical development and health, therefore, adults need to pay close attention to what children are capable of and what skills may be emerging:

At planning time, Zachary says he is going to play basketball. As work time begins, he puts a small basket on top of a shelf in the block area and tries to throw foam balls into it. After several misses, Zachary tells his teacher, "It's too hard!" "How could you make it easier?" she asks him. Zachary thinks for a minute and says, "I could stand closer." He moves closer to the basket and the next ball goes in. "That's a three-pointer," he tells the teacher.

At the end of afternoon snacktime, Gigi wipes crumbs from her place with a wet paper towel. There are still several crumbs and some spilled juice left on the table as Gigi joins the other children on the rug for large-group time before they leave for the day. Gigi's teacher waits until the children have gone before thoroughly cleaning the table and the floor underneath it.

As children develop new skills, it's important for adults to keep their expectations reasonable, as do the teachers in the preceding examples. Don't expect children to perform at the level of adults or to demonstrate the skills and knowledge of older children. (The scaffolding charts in the next five chapters provide many examples of the range of behaviors you can reasonably expect in each skill area.) Encourage and appreciate children's attempts to do things, rather than judging the outcomes according to the standards you hold for yourself. To be a *supportive model and guide* for children as their physical skills and healthy behaviors emerge, use the ideas that follow.

Provide cues to encourage children's success as they attempt new skills

Cues are small bits of information that can help children learn or enhance a skill. Encourage children to explore movements on their own first, and offer cues only if they appear frustrated or are eager to advance but are unsure of how to do so. Cues can be *verbal* (telling a child who keeps falling off a balance beam, "Try holding your hands out to the side"); *visual*

With the adult providing hands-on guidance, the child climbs and reaches for the apple on his own.

(demonstrating holding your arms out to the side for balance); or, with the child's permission, *hands-on* (gently centering the child's body over the balance beam). Individualize the type of cue(s) you use, depending on what each child is most receptive to.

Model movements and healthy behaviors

Carrying out an action yourself while using the same equipment or materials as children provides low-key assistance without explicit directions. This strategy can be especially useful for children with limited receptive vocabulary.

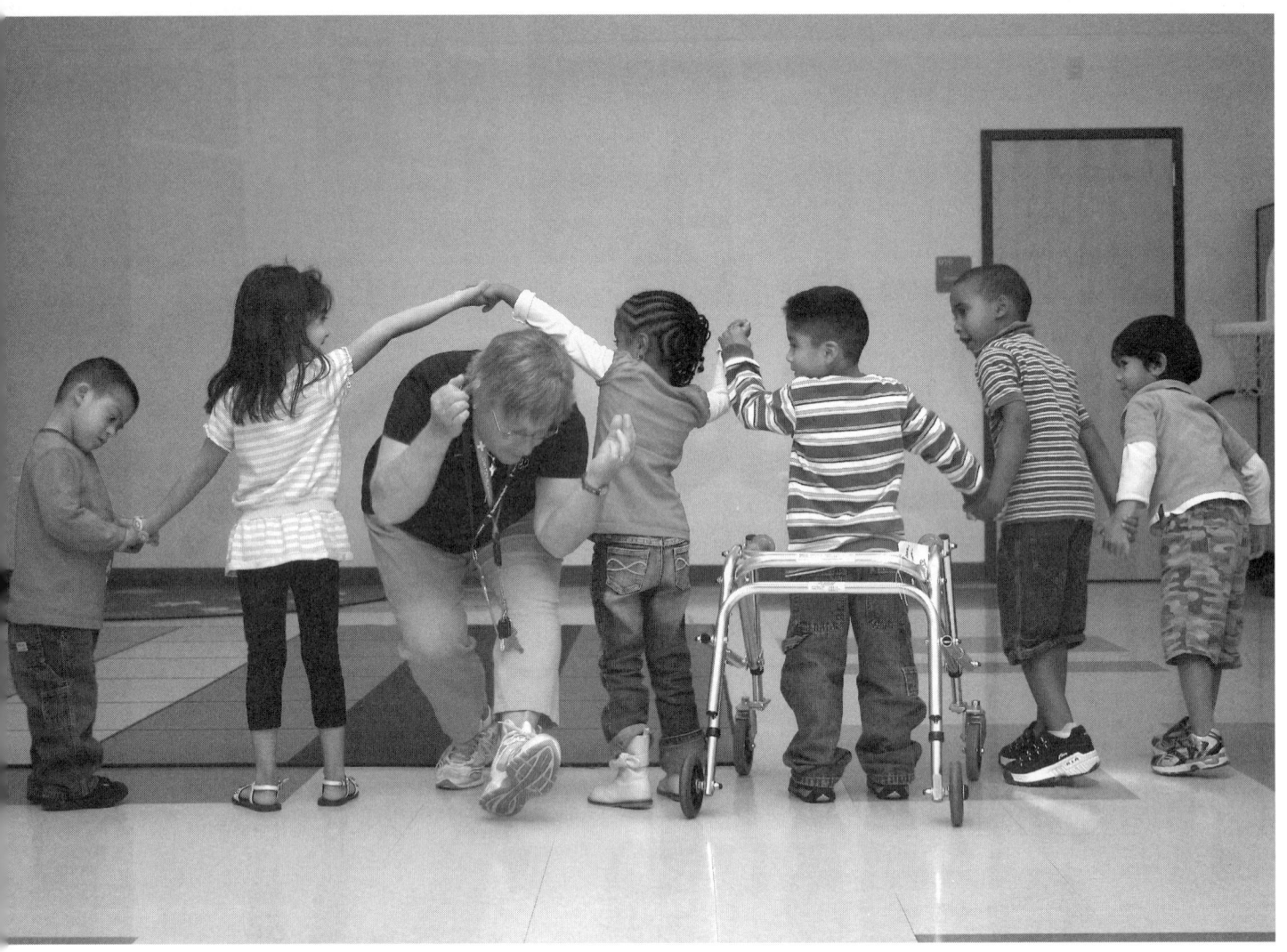

As she works with children who have various special needs, this adult models and guides the skills needed for a movement game.

The goal of modeling is not for children to copy you exactly, but to get the idea and then practice on their own. You can also serve as a model for self-help skills and healthy habits. For example, a child whose coat fastens the same way as yours can see how you use two hands to slip a button into its hole. When you eat an apple and comment "I like to eat an apple every day — it tastes good and it's full of vitamins and minerals," you are serving as a model for healthy nutrition. You can also show your interest in trying new foods, for example, when families share favorite dishes from home. Again, don't expect (and never require) children to try them too, but be a model for curiosity and adventurousness in physical and health-related behaviors.

Create challenges

Gentle challenges can sustain children's interest in practicing a skill or adopting a healthy habit. "Challenges are tasks or activities made measurable (or more fun) by the teacher. In making a task measurable, the teacher motivates a child to try it in a different way" (Sanders, 2002, p. 55).

Remember that challenges should motivate, not frustrate, the child. Keep them achievable and never make them competitive. For example, if a child is bouncing a ball, you might say, "I wonder how many different ways you can bounce it." Or say to a small group of children, "I wonder how many fruits we can think of" and, together with them, exclaim with pleasure at the length of the list you record. Note how the teacher in the following example suggests an achievable challenge that builds on play children are already engaged in:

At outside time, several children use chalk to draw a hopscotch board of connected squares on the pavement, then hop from square to square. Other children join in, adding numbers to the squares and drawing more connected boxes. After several days of observing the children enjoying this game, their teacher draws some boxes that are not connected. "These are leaping boxes," she remarks to Kenneth, who is watching her, "because the boxes are so far apart you have to leap between them." The children are eager to try them. At the end of the day, Kenneth tells his mother, "Guess what! Now we play 'hopscotch' and 'leapscotch'!"

Add language to describe behavior related to physical development and health

With encouragement and support from adults, children can be surprisingly articulate about their physical and health-related accomplishments and knowledge:

At outside time, Brian says to his teacher, "Look, I was down low and now I'm standing up." She replies, "You were crouching down low and now you're standing up high."

❖

Operating the apple peeler is a physical challenge posed by the adult, who makes it more achievable by steadying the peeler while the child does the work.

At large-group time, Ms. Moore says to Jamaica, "You're wiggling your feet." Jamaica says, "Watch! I can wiggle them real fast!"

❖

While getting ready for outside time, Cole claims with pride, "I did my button!" Demitra, his teacher, acknowledges, "You slipped the button into the hole all by yourself!"

❖

At snacktime, the teacher says, "These grapes are sweet and juicy. They squirt inside my mouth." The children talk about how much juice is in other fruits they like to eat. "My husband laughs when the juice dribbles down my chin," the teacher tells them.

At recall time, if this child refers to his play with the large ball, the teacher might encourage him to describe how he used his hands to move the ball. This will help the child develop a movement vocabulary and awareness of specific kinds of movement.

Describing children's movements and health-related behaviors serves a dual purpose. It makes them more aware of specific aspects of their physical actions and health-related behaviors, for example, which body part they are moving, how they are moving, their spatial relations (where they and the objects they are using are in relation to one another), and how and what they are doing to take care of themselves. Verbal labels also increase their vocabulary. When they hear adults use new words (sometimes after many repetitions), children can begin to think about the concepts and use the words themselves. This helps them master new challenges; for example, a child who understands putting one foot *in front of* the other can use a verbal cue to do so when learning to throw a ball. Children can also apply physical terms to other areas of learning. For example, words such as *beginning/end*, *top/bottom*, *fast/slow*, or *straight/bent* reflect concepts related to literacy, mathematics, and the creative arts.

Adults should also encourage children to describe their own gross- and fine-motor movements, as well as to share their thoughts on personal care and healthy behaviors. For example, listen to and repeat what children say as they incorporate movements into their play. Encourage them to use movement terms when they plan and recall. When they choose to be the leader at large-group time, encourage them to describe as well as demonstrate their movements to the other children. The following are some examples of children's descriptions of their movements and the ways teachers encourage this language:

At outside time, Christy says to her teacher, "It went up behind me!" Her teacher replies, "The ball went up and came down behind you." Christy adds, "It went backward," and her teacher comments, "It went backward when you hit it."

❖

At planning time, Dante says he's going to make a ramp with the big blocks and see how far he can jump off the end.

❖

At work time, Aimee asks Chelsea to show her how to tie her shoe. "First, go like this," Chelsea says. She grasps a lace in each hand and waits for Aimee to do the same. "Now turn this one around this one and pull." She pauses while Aimee imitates this movement and says, "Then bend it,…go around,…and push this one through for the other loop. …Then pull…and there!"

❖

At large-group time when it is Kenneth's turn to be the leader, he waves his arms when the music stops. "You're waving your arms above your head," says his teacher. "Yes," says Kenneth. "Let's do it Kenneth's way," the teacher says. "Everybody wave their arms in the air when the music stops."

❖

At recall time, Erin says she rubbed soap on the baby doll, dunked it in the bowl, and patted it dry with a towel. After snacktime, several children "pat" the table dry with paper towels.

Key Developmental Indicators in Physical Development and Health

HighScope has five **key developmental indicators (KDIs)** in Physical Development and Health: 16. Gross-motor skills, 17. Fine-motor skills, 18. Body awareness, 19. Personal care, and 20. Healthy behavior. See the chart on the next page for a full description of each KDI.

The five KDIs in Physical Development and Health help adults understand the abilities that are developing in children's everyday behaviors.

Key Developmental Indicators in Physical Development and Health

C. Physical Development and Health

16. Gross-motor skills: Children demonstrate strength, flexibility, balance, and timing in using their large muscles.
Description: Children use nonlocomotor (stationary) movements (e.g., bending, twisting, rocking) and locomotor (traveling) movements (e.g., walking, climbing, running, jumping, hopping, skipping, marching, galloping). They coordinate gross-motor movements in throwing, catching, kicking, bouncing balls, and using a swing.

17. Fine-motor skills: Children demonstrate dexterity and hand-eye coordination in using their small muscles.
Description: Children use the fine-motor movements (e.g., molding, squeezing, poking, smoothing, positioning, writing, cutting) needed to manipulate materials and tools. They have hand-eye coordination (e.g., stacking blocks, assembling puzzles, stringing beads, pouring juice, pounding nails).

18. Body awareness: Children know about their bodies and how to navigate them in space.
Description: Children recognize the names and locations of body parts. They are aware of their own bodies in relation to people and objects around them. Children feel, and move their bodies to, a steady beat.

19. Personal care: Children carry out personal care routines on their own.
Description: Children feed themselves, dress, wash their hands, brush their teeth, use tissues, and use the toilet.

20. Healthy behavior: Children engage in healthy practices.
Description: Children participate in active, physical play. They know that some foods are healthier than others. Children carry out behaviors that are healthy (e.g., cough into their elbow, wash their hands after toileting, use their own fork) and safe (e.g., wear a bike helmet, not walk in front of a moving swing, walk around a spill).

Chapters 3 to 7 discuss the knowledge and skills young children acquire in each of these KDIs and the specific teaching strategies adults can use to support this learning. Each chapter concludes with a "scaffolding chart" containing examples of what children might say and do at early, middle, and later stages of development and how adults can scaffold their learning through appropriate support and gentle extensions. In addition to the ideas detailed in the text, these charts offer additional ideas on how you might carry out the strategies in the following chapters during play and other interactions with the children.

CHAPTER 3

KDI 16. Gross-Motor Skills

C. Physical Development and Health
16. Gross-motor skills: Children demonstrate strength, flexibility, balance, and timing in using their large muscles.

Description: Children use nonlocomotor (stationary) movements (e.g., bending, twisting, rocking) and locomotor (traveling) movements (e.g., walking, climbing, running, jumping, hopping, skipping, marching, galloping). They coordinate gross-motor movements in throwing, catching, kicking, bouncing balls, and using a swing.

At large-group time, Ella shows the other children how to jump up and down "like scissors," alternating which leg lands in front and which leg lands behind.

❖

At outside time, David hits a foam ball with a plastic bat as his teacher pitches it to him.

❖

While pretending to be a dog at work time, Curtis stands on the top stair, jumps down to the floor (four stairs), and crawls around barking.

❖

At large-group time, Claire suggests leaps around the circle for musical chairs.

Changes in physical growth during the preschool years, especially the lowering of the child's center of gravity,[3] make for steadier and more sure-footed movements (Tomlinson & Hyson, 2009). Young children are increasingly able to use their limbs for activities such as running, jumping, and climbing. However, because their nervous system and musculature are still not fully mature, preschoolers' reaction time is generally slower than that of early elementary-age children. The rate of maturation is affected by several factors, including genetics, temperamental dispositions, environmental opportunities, and adult support. Variations in ability mean that, to adults, preschoolers sometimes appear uncoordinated or kinesthetically unaware; yet as Stephen Sanders points out, "from a young child's point of view, participating in daily physical activity is simply a fun way to learn and grow" (2002, p. xiv).

How Gross-Motor Skills Develop

Preschoolers develop several types of gross-motor skills. **Nonlocomotor** or **anchored movements** are performed in personal space without moving around and involve "movements of the upper and lower body…that do not result in transferring weight from one foot to the other foot" (Weikart, 2000, p. 19). Examples include tapping the head while sitting, swaying side to side or rocking back

---

[3]Infants' heads are large relative to the rest of their bodies, giving them a higher center of gravity. As children enter toddlerhood, the lower part of their bodies acquires more weight and their center of gravity shifts downward. They are less likely to topple over head first, and more likely to land on their bottoms — a safety feature supplied by nature as children become more mobile. As their body proportions and weight continue to balance out, preschoolers become increasingly steady and also more flexible in how and where they can move their bodies.

Nonlocomotor movements are movements of the arms, legs, trunk, or head performed while anchored in place.

Locomotor movements are traveling movements or movements that involve a weight transfer.

and forth in place, bending and straightening the arms, or twisting the upper body while the feet remain in position on the floor. **Locomotor** or **nonanchored movements** involve a weight transfer or moving through space. Basic locomotor skills include walking, marching, running, galloping, and jumping, or any of these movements performed in place. Here are two more examples of simple nonlocomotor and locomotor movement:

At large-group time, Aimee bends her arms and flaps her elbows against her sides. Petey watches Aimee, then tries the same motions with his elbows. (Nonlocomotor movement)

At recall time, Mikey jumps to all the places where he played during work time. (Locomotor movement)

As with many other types of development, both nonlocomotor and locomotor skills progress from simple to complex. In addition to the basic developmental sequences shown in the chart on the next page, both nonlocomotor and locomotor movement become more complex when performed *with objects*. For example, while standing in place (nonlocomotor movement), a child can throw a beanbag, kick a ball, or tap with rhythm sticks. Likewise, a child can traverse space (locomotor movement) by walking in a circle while waving paper plates,

Developmental Progressions in Nonlocomotor and Locomotor Movement

Nonlocomotor movement

This chart presents the basic nonlocomotor movements (movements without weight transfers), showing the progression from the simplest to the most complex movements.

SIMPLE ──────> MORE COMPLEX

Two-sided symmetrical movements
- **Action-word movements** — Movements children describe in single words

    Examples: pound, shake, wiggle

- **Basic single movements** — Specific movements described in standard single words

    Examples: twist, swing, turn, rock

- **Sequenced movements**

    Examples: bend/straighten, push/pull, open/close

One-side/other-side movements
Example: swinging one arm several times, then swinging the other arm several times (while holding the non-swinging arm still)

Alternating movements
Example: swinging arms back and forth with one arm forward, the other arm back

Locomotor movement

This chart presents the basic locomotor movements (movements with weight transfers), showing the progression from the simplest to the most complex movements.

SIMPLE ──────> MORE COMPLEX

Alternating single movements
Examples: crawling, walking, marching, running, galloping, sliding (sideways gallop). Skipping is an example of an alternating locomotor movement that is more complex.

Two-sided movements
Example: jumping

One-side/other-side movements
Example: hopping on one foot for several repetitions, then hopping on the other foot for several repetitions.

— Adapted from *Moving With Purpose* by K. S. Sawyers with E. Colley and L. Icaza (2010, pp. 22, 24)

Movements with objects are more demanding for preschoolers than basic movements carried out without objects.

❖

Dawson walks around the room balancing a plastic circle from the shape-sorter game on his head. (Locomotor movement with objects)

In the course of developing gross-motor skills, young children also explore and construct **movement concepts** (Graham, Holt/Hale, & Parker, 2004; Sanders, 2002). They develop **spatial awareness** (understanding location, position, and direction) as they observe people and objects moving through the environment. **Effort awareness** is recognizing the energy (force) and time it takes to carry out movements, while **body or relational awareness** is seeing how bodies (or parts of bodies) move in relation to other people and the space around them (see KDI 18. Body awareness). If we think of movement *skills* as relating to what the body can do, then movement *concepts* relate to children's understanding of how and where the body moves. Learning and using movement concepts helps young children modify the range and improve the effectiveness of their movement skills. That is, by understanding the principles underlying various large-motor actions, children can bring more intentionality and purpose to their movements.

by gliding with a scarf, or by marching with a drum.[4] Here are two more examples of moving with objects:

At work time, Bonita and Manuel sit on the couch and rock the "babies" (dolls) in their arms to sleep. (Nonlocomotor movement with objects)

One group of children became very interested in dropping scarves from the climber and were quite amazed at how slowly they drifted to the ground. "It takes a long time for them to go down," one child noted. This observation led the children to try out being "slow scarves" during large group, in which they exhibited an understanding and tolerance for moving slowly, a capacity they had not shown before. (Epstein, 2007, p. 101)

---

[4]Some movement educators use the terms *stability skills, locomotor skills,* and *manipulative skills* to describe these three types of movement (Gallahue, 1995; Sanders, 2002). In stability skills (as in nonlocomotor movement), the body remains in place but moves around its horizontal or vertical axis. In locomotor skills, the body is transported in a horizontal or vertical direction from one point in space to another. Manipulative skills involve giving force to objects or receiving force from objects (as in moving with objects).

Teaching Strategies That Support Gross-Motor Skills

Adults can encourage the development of gross-motor skills in young children by using the teaching strategies described here.

Encourage children to explore a wide range of positions and movements

To support children in exploring positions, play position games with children, such as statues, in which children move until the leader says the word *freeze* or stops the music. Encourage children to be the leader and have others imitate the poses they strike. Describe and encourage the children to describe their positions in words and phrases, such as arms *up over* the head, leg *to the side*, body *bent over* at the waist). Children can also try to make the same movement from different positions, for example, lying on their backs or their sides while lifting their legs.

To encourage exploration of nonlocomotor movements, ask children to think of all the ways they can move their arms, legs, head, or torso while remaining stationary (see "Body Positions for Nonlocomotor Movement," p. 38, for suggestions for stationary starting positions for these explorations). For example, children might stand in place and swing their arms to music at large-group time, or pretend to be trees bending in the wind or stretching their "branches" up to the sky. They also will enjoy rocking dolls in the house area. Not only is it satisfying to children to comfort their "babies," but the steady movement can be soothing to the rocker as well. Outside time also offers possibilities for nonlocomotor movement. Although we commonly think of the outdoors as a place to move vigorously from one location to another, children also enjoy many in-place movements while outside. For example, they like to observe shadows or feel the changes in air current as they twist back and forth or bob their heads up and down.

> "Children truly enjoy exploring movements initiated by an adult, another child, or themselves. Providing appropriate adult encouragement and support not only enables young children to learn about movement but also ensures the success of their many movement ideas and experiences."
>
> — Weikart (2000, p. 28)

Games like statues, in which children freeze in place at a signal and are asked to describe their movements, enable children to explore body positions and attach vocabulary to them.

KDI 16. Gross-Motor Skills 37

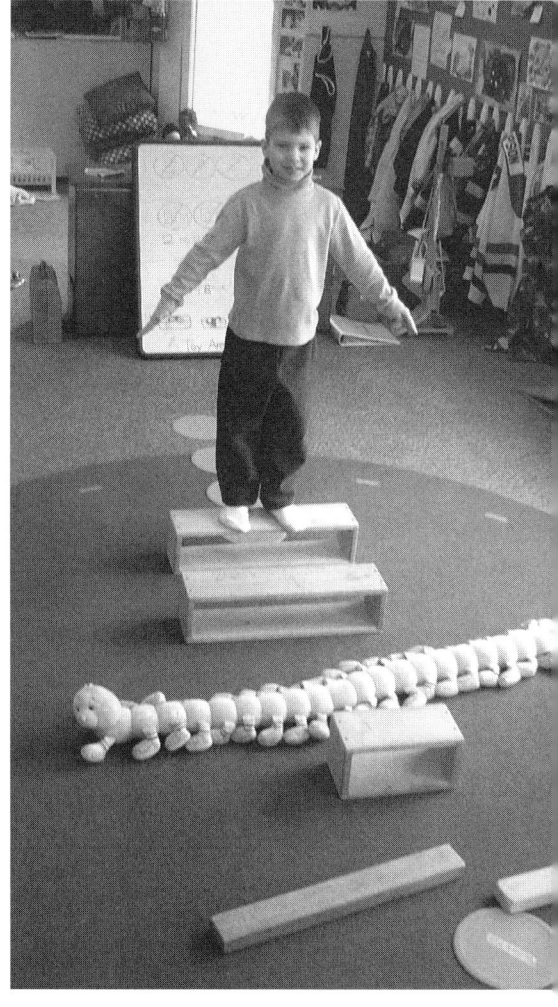

In the spacious, open block area in this classroom, children often build large block structures and use them for climbing on and experimenting with various movements and body positions. Sometimes they enclose the space with a block boundary and use the space inside to explore movements on the floor.

> **Body Positions for Nonlocomotor Movement**
>
> "The body positions that may be used in exploring nonlocomotor movement are as follows:
> - Lying on one's back (supine position)
> - Lying on one's stomach (prone position)
> - Lying on one's side (side position)
> - Sitting down with legs straight in front, or in a 'V' shape in front of the body, or folded close to the body
> - Kneeling on hands and knees, just on the knees, or curled into a ball
> - Standing with feet close together or with feet apart"
>
> — Weikart (2000, p. 68)

To provide opportunities for practicing locomotor movements, plan activities in which children can run, jump, and use other active motions. These can take place during small- and large-group time, outside time, and transitions. For example, for a large-group activity, create an obstacle course with blocks, carpet squares, shelves, ramps, chairs, tables, and tape marks on the floor. Invite children to help plan and construct it. To encourage children to try a variety of locomotor movements during transitions, designate pathways to move from one activity to another (e.g., from the table to the sink after lunch or from area to area as they put away toys at cleanup). Suggest ways children can move along the pathway, and ask them to contribute their own ideas. Ruth Strubank (1991) describes how teachers can use this strategy as children move from planning time to work time: "The teacher lays a 'planning path' (made from long sheets of fabric) on the floor and asks children to choose a way to move their bodies along the path (e.g., crawl, hop, go backwards, jump, walk like a crab) to an area where they plan to work" (p. 106).

The strategy of asking children for movement ideas for the group to imitate often leads to creative and varied suggestions:

At large-group time, Alex shows how to creep across the floor for the other children to copy. Some crawl on their knees, other creep with their stomachs flat on the ground.

❖

At large-group time, Eli demonstrates "twirling in a circle" as a way for the group to move their bodies. Later, at snacktime, Eli says he wants to jump during the next large-group time.

Spontaneous opportunities for children to hop, leap, gallop, and move their bodies in other ways also arise at work time.

Children enjoy discovering the full range of nonlocomotor (stationary) and locomotor (traveling) movements their bodies can make. Provide opportunities for them to investigate their large-motor capacities and challenge themselves throughout the day.

Encourage children to build movement skills in sequence

As Heather Tomlinson and Marilou Hyson point out, "As in other domains, children move through a sequence of refining their gross-motor skills" (2009, p. 116). Preschoolers work up to a more complex movement by gradually mastering its components. For example, take the skill of learning how to strike an object. Children are more apt to feel successful when they have the opportunity to move through the following sequence: (1) use their hands to strike stationary objects such as a balloon placed on a table

Striking a ball placed on a cone builds readiness for the more complex task of striking a ball in the air.

or tee; (2) strike at an object suspended from a string or rope; (3) strike at an object dropped in front of them; and (4) strike at an object gently thrown to them. Likewise, it helps to sequence the objects used for striking. Begin with something that has a large, flat striking surface like a paddle or racket. Save long-handled objects with narrow striking surfaces (like bats or golf clubs) for last, since these items call for estimating distance *and* coordinating physical movement.

Sequencing also applies when children are learning to follow movement directions. Begin with one movement at a time and let children practice it for a while (e.g., pat the head). Add a second movement (e.g., pat the head and touch the shoulders) only after they are comfortable and confident with the first one. Keep each movement simple and familiar. Encourage children to suggest pairs of movements, and to use words as well as gestures to demonstrate the movements. Preschoolers also find it easier to follow movement directions if you separate the verbal and visual components (Weikart, 2000). Begin by demonstrating a movement without talking *or* by describing it in words without moving. Then ask the children to try it. They may differ in which type of cue is most effective for them (verbal or visual), so alternate these approaches when giving directions. After they master a movement, you can combine the verbal and visual components the next time you give directions. Here are examples of teachers using these strategies, singly or in combination, to give directions for single and sequenced movements:

At large-group time, the teacher says, "Watch and copy." She pats her head without saying a word.

❖

At large-group time, the teacher stands still and says, "Tap your shoulders."

❖

At large-group time, the teacher says, "Watch me." He begins marching in place, and the children join in. After the children have been marching for a while, he begins to chant, "March, march, march, march," and some of the children join in the chant.

❖

At large-group time, the teacher pats her nose with both hands and then pats her ears. The children copy her. Then the teacher adds the words "nose, ears, nose, ears" as she and the children continue to pat. After many repetitions, she asks the children to name two places to pat. Jason touches his eyes and chin, and everyone imitates his movements. When it is Katya's turn, she says, "Nose and cheek" and the class pats the two places she has named.

Using no words, a teacher demonstrates a movement for children to imitate. Note that one child is watching intently but not yet doing the movement. This makes it easier for her to process the visual instructions.

The importance of exploration in the sequence of mastering movement skills cannot be overstated. Young children need to explore what their bodies can do and how they can move with objects before they attempt to master specific skills such as jumping, throwing a beanbag, or swatting a ball. Note, for example, how Fenton explores the process of striking while using materials he picked up outdoors:

At outside time, Fenton uses a stick to knock a piece of bark off the edge of the picnic table. He repeats this action over and over, each time placing the bark farther from the edge.

Giving children time and materials for exploration also provides teachers with opportunities to observe children's level of motor development and plan appropriate supporting activities. Moreover, when adults make comments about children's exploratory movements, they acknowledge their efforts and give other children ideas they might be interested in exploring as well. Encouraging children to try doing something a different way (or with a new material, as in the next example), may also expand their creativity:

At work time in the block area, Lily throws beanbags into a wide-mouthed basket. The beanbags land in the basket about a third of the time. The next day at small-group time the teacher gives the children containers with different-sized openings, along with balls and beanbags to throw into them. For several days afterwards, Lily practices throwing different objects into small- and wide-mouthed containers.

Provide interesting materials to accompany children's movements

Think of equipment and materials that children can move with, move on (under, inside, and around), and make move. (In addition to the suggestions that follow, see the list of gross-motor materials on pp. 46–47.)

Things to move with. Young children may feel more secure if they hold onto things while trying out new movements. They also enjoy seeing how their movements affect the objects they hold. For example, they can notice how a pinwheel turns, a carton of water ripples, or a strip of paper waves as they "skate" with it across the room. Other ideas for novel objects children can move with include paper fans, chopsticks, strips of jingling bells or shells, and closed containers filled with sound-making materials such as pebbles and beads. Children's uses of such materials and their comments about what happens are often inventive and unexpected:

At large-group time, Alicia uses the rhythm sticks as she imitates a scraping motion. She holds one stick in one hand and rubs the other one up and down along it.

❖

At outside time, the children carry buckets of water from the spigot to the garden. Sean observes that when he moves "a little fast," the water "wiggles" on the surface. Wendy races across the yard and says "Oops!" when the water splashes over the edge. After she slows down, she looks in the bucket and comments, "Now it's not doing anything."

Things to move on. Once children master basic large-motor movements, they are free to become interested in how and where their feet can move. Preschoolers enjoy moving on or inside of different things, such as sliding their feet atop paper plates, walking with their feet in boxes or adult-size shoes or with tin cans strapped underneath them, or rolling dowels ahead of their toes:

At outside time, Nathaniel brings a large rubber ball back to the shed. He sits on it while rolling it underneath him. Then he stands up and kicks it the rest of the way with his feet. His first kick is hard and sends the ball past the shed. He brings the ball back to his starting point and gives it small, easy kicks until he reaches the shed's door. Then he sits on it again and rides the ball inside, rolling it beneath him.

In addition to moving *on* things, there are many items that children can use to move inside of, over or under, around, and so on (see the suggestion for creating an obstacle course, p. 38). Preschoolers enjoy crawling in and out of "caves" they've made by draping sheets over a table. Large metal drums with both ends removed and filed smooth make good tunnels to crawl through. Big boxes, such as those from household appliances, are another attraction that children enjoy navigating in various ways. (Appliance stores and families are often happy to donate empty cartons.) Children enjoy slipping through the flaps, stretching out inside or alongside, and trying different ways to get their bodies over and around these oversized containers.

Things to make move. Provide materials for tossing, throwing, kicking, striking, and catching. Since the bouncing motion of rubber balls is sometimes difficult for preschoolers to handle, offer alternatives that can be used in similar ways (pompoms, beanbags, balls of yarn,

Materials to Accompany Children's Movements

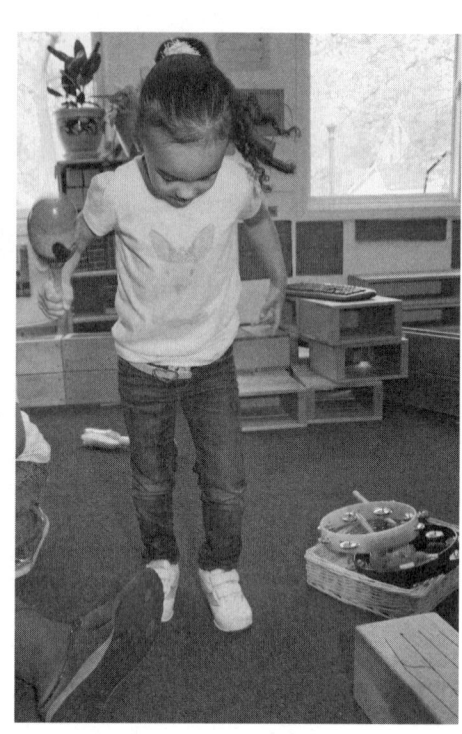

Things to move with, *such as hoops and a pair of maracas, help these children maintain their balance and learn to coordinate the movements of their hands, arms, and trunk with those of their legs and feet.*

Things to move on, *such as paper plates on the floor and a portable ramp, help children develop awareness of where their bodies are moving in relation to other people and objects.*

KDI 16. Gross-Motor Skills   43

Things to make move, *such as sleds, balls of many sizes, and a wagon, provide a variety of thrills and challenges for children playing alone or with others.*

balled socks, and foam balls). Floating objects such as scarves can also be thrown in the air; they return to earth slowly enough for children to catch, kick, or strike them. Containers that make easy targets, such as large cardboard boxes or laundry tubs, are also good for practicing these movement skills. When you do use balls with preschoolers, make sure they are large and lightweight. Broad plastic bats and boards to practice hitting such objects are also appropriate. Here are some more examples of how child-friendly materials promote children's successes with these skills:

At outside time, Joel throws a plastic ball in the air and hits it with a bat.

❖

At outside time, Donna hits a ball off the top of an orange cone with a bat.

❖

At large-group time, while moving to the music, Mimi throws a scarf up and over her head, then catches the scarf as it floats down.

Preschoolers also enjoy large items they can push and pull, such as wagons, wheelbarrows, carriages, and tires; big blocks for building; and big boxes and baskets they can use to transport people and objects. These large play items serve several needs. Children develop strength and coordination maneuvering them around the room or playground. Also, because big equipment often requires more than one person to manage, it can help promote collaboration between children:

At work time, Kerry and Gillian play with the racing cars. Zeke hangs around nearby, wanting to join them but not sure how to enter their play.

When Kerry says, "We need the big boards to build a race track," Zeke offers, "I can help carry them." "Come on," says Gillian. Zeke and Gillian carry the boards to the center of the room, each holding one end. As Gillian and Zeke fetch more, Kerry tells them where to put the boards and line them up.

Provide children with experiences and materials for exploring movement concepts

Provide children with experiences that allow them to explore the weight and force of their movements. Comment on their level of effort (e.g., "Lucy carried that heavy box all the way across the room!"). Ask children to pretend to carry things of different weights. For example, say, "Let's imagine we're lifting a hammer over our heads. Now pretend it's a feather from a tiny bird." Use large balls made of materials of different weights, such as lightweight plastic and heavy rubber, and encourage children to comment on how hard or easy it is for them to kick the balls across the grass. You can also give children hard and soft materials to transform, and comment on how much effort it takes. For example, they can compare hammering nails into wood versus pounding golf tees into Styrofoam (remember to use safety goggles and take other appropriate precautions). In this example, children encounter various movement concepts as they work with hoops:

At large-group time, everyone has a hoop. "I know," says Joey. "Let's have one foot in and one foot out." After the children try walking around their hoops this way, the teacher suggests, "Let's try that again, but this time we could be very strong *and stamp our feet as we walk." The children walk around their hoops, stamping one foot in and one foot out of the circle.*

Commenting on children's physical feats ("Looks like you two have teamed up to carry the heavy block") helps children gain understanding of movement concepts involving force and effort.

For examples of how young children develop gross-motor skills and how adults can support and gently extend their learning at different levels, see "Ideas for Scaffolding KDI 16. Gross-Motor Skills" on page 48. Use the ideas in the chart, in addition to those described earlier, to scaffold children's gross-motor skills during play and other interactions.

Materials for Gross-Motor Movement[5]

Large building materials
- Large hollow blocks, ramps, boards
- Cardboard blocks
- Blocks made from boxes or milk cartons, covered with cloth or contact paper
- Pieces of carpet, cardboard, Plexiglas, Styrofoam
- Sheets, blankets, tarps, tents
- Packing boxes
- Boards, sticks, logs, stumps, and tree-stump rounds
- Large cardboard, metal, or plastic tubes
- Rope and pulleys
- Obstacle course materials: ramps, appliance boxes, things to move on, over, and through

Movement activity props
- Scarves, ribbons
- Hoops
- Limbo sticks
- Paper plates
- Strips of jingling bells or shells
- Musical instruments to march with
- Shakers with sound-making materials

Wheeled toys
- Tricycles
- Scooters
- Wagons
- Wheelbarrow
- Push vehicles with steering wheels
- Strollers, carriages

Loose materials for the outdoors
- Jumping equipment
  - Inner tubes, trampolines
  - Old mattress
  - Ropes (to jump over)
- Equipment for throwing, kicking, and aiming
  - Balls (all sizes)
  - Beanbags
  - Low basketball hoop and net
  - Pails, buckets, boxes, bull's-eye targets
- Building materials
  - Boards of varying lengths
  - Slotted plywood pieces (sanded smooth)
  - Styrofoam sheets, boards, packing pieces
  - Cardboard boxes
  - Twine, rope, pulleys
  - Old sheets, blankets, tarps
  - Small sawhorses
  - Tires, inner tubes
  - Workbench and tools

---
[5]Check local licensing regulations and agencies and organizations such as the Consumer Product Safety Commission (www.cpsc.gov), the American Academy of Pediatrics (www.aap.org), and the National Resource Center for Health and Safety in Child Care and Early Education (www.nrckids.org) for current information on product safety.

KDI 16. Gross-Motor Skills

Stationary outdoor structures
- Climbers
  - Jungle gym, net climber
  - Trees with low branches close together
- High places
  - Raised platform, low tree house, sturdy crates
  - Hills, boulders
  - Tree stumps, snow piles
- Swings
  - Commercial swing set, multiperson tire swing
  - Rope swing from tree, low hammock
  - Spring-based rocking toys
- Slides
  - Commercial slide, hill slide
  - Low ramp, low cable ride
  - Firefighter's pole, sleds for winter
- Balances
  - Balance beams
  - Rows of railroad ties, bricks, or rocks arranged in rows (including parallel rows, curving, and zigzag rows)

- Sand and water materials
  - Sand pit, box, table or tubs
  - Sand, pea gravel, shells, wood shavings, leaves, pine cones, snow
  - Wading pool, spigot, hose, hand pump, flexible tubing
  - Large shovels, buckets
- Large outdoor art materials
  - Painting canvases made from old sheets, paints
  - Paint rollers, large brushes
  - Bubbles and bubble wands
  - Large-scale weaving frame or fence to weave on
  - Large-size multicolored chalk
  - Clay for imprints of grass, stones, leaves, etc.
  - Food coloring, sand tools, boxes, cans for snow sculpture

Ideas for Scaffolding KDI 16. Gross-Motor Skills

Always support children at their current level and occasionally offer a gentle extension.

Earlier	Middle	Later
Children may	*Children may*	*Children may*
• Do single nonlocomotor movements (e.g., swing, turn, shake, or twist).	• Do two nonlocomotor movements in sequence (e.g., bend and straighten, push and pull).	• Repeat three or more nonlocomotor movements in sequence (e.g., pat knees, pat shoulders, pat head, and repeat).
• Do simple locomotor movements (e.g., walk, climb, run).	• Do or attempt complex locomotor movements (e.g., jump, gallop).	• Do complex locomotor movements with ease and coordination (e.g., hop, skip).
• Manipulate objects while staying in place (e.g., stand behind a ball and kick it; extend arms to the front and try to catch a beanbag by trapping it against the chest).	• Manipulate objects while moving (e.g., take two or three deliberate steps before kicking a ball).	• Manipulate objects while staying in place or moving with ease and coordination (e.g., tap rhythm sticks to the beat of a chant or musical selection; throw a ball in the air and run underneath to catch it).
To support children's current level, adults can	*To support children's current level, adults can*	*To support children's current level, adults can*
• Imitate and label the children's single nonlocomotor movements (e.g., "I'm going to try swinging my arms too").	• Acknowledge and label children's nonlocomotor movement sequences.	• Provide opportunities for children to do movement sequences (e.g., while awaiting lunch, have children pat table, clap hands, and flick fingers, then repeat).
• Imitate and label the children's simple locomotor movements (e.g., "I wonder if I can march like you").	• Do and label complex locomotor movements alongside children (e.g., jump or gallop and say what you are doing); accept the ways that children move.	• Acknowledge children's complex locomotor movements (e.g., "You hopped on one foot and then the other").
• Acknowledge when children manipulate objects while staying in place (e.g., "You stood behind the ball and then you kicked it").	• Imitate and describe how children manipulate objects while moving (e.g., "I'm taking two steps and kicking the ball just like you did").	• Provide opportunities for children to manipulate a variety of objects while staying in place or moving.
To offer a gentle extension, adults can	*To offer a gentle extension, adults can*	*To offer a gentle extension, adults can*
• Call attention to how other children are moving in similar ways (e.g., "You're twisting your waist. Marissa is twisting her arm").	• Ask children to describe their movement sequences (e.g., "What do you call it when you move your arm like this and then like that?").	• Challenge children to add to their movement sequence (e.g., "We touched our knees and then our shoulders. What can we do next?").
• Add a variation to children's simple locomotor movement (e.g., "Let's march with our knees high").	• Provide opportunities for children to do complex locomotor movements.	• Ask children to describe their complex locomotor movements.
• Ask children how else they could manipulate an object while staying in place (e.g., "You've been catching the beanbag. I wonder what else you could do with it").	• Encourage children to think of other ways to use objects while moving (e.g., "How else could we move with our shakers?").	• Give children opportunities to manipulate similar objects while moving (e.g., "You've been running and kicking the big ball. Here are some smaller balls to try").

CHAPTER 4

KDI 17. Fine-Motor Skills

C. Physical Development and Health
17. Fine-motor skills: Children demonstrate dexterity and hand-eye coordination in using their small muscles.

Description: Children use the fine-motor movements (e.g., molding, squeezing, poking, smoothing, positioning, writing, cutting) needed to manipulate materials and tools. They have hand-eye coordination (e.g., stacking blocks, assembling puzzles, stringing beads, pouring juice, pounding nails).

At work time in the house area, Joey uses both hands to put a dress, socks, hat, and bib on the doll. He buttons the dress, wraps the elastic hat band around the doll's chin, and overlaps the straps on the bib to tie it in back.

❖

At work time in the art area, Jayla turns the piece of paper she is cutting with one hand as she uses the scissors with her other hand.

❖

At work time in the house area, Kovid says he is making a tortilla with the play dough. He gets a rolling pin and, grasping it with both hands, says, "I have to roll it flat." He pats and rolls the dough into a flat circle.

❖

At recall time, the children twirl a spinner to show what area they played in.

Preschoolers are making great strides in using their hands and fingers, which in turn allows them to carry out their ideas and accomplish the tasks they set for themselves.

Young children gain strength, flexibility, and hand-eye coordination as they manipulate objects. They can take things apart and put them back together, fit small objects into holes, align things in parallel rows, stack blocks and other flat objects so they balance, sort small objects, fold big pieces of paper or fabric into smaller ones, do simple fingerplays, begin to write letters and numbers, and create drawings or sculptures that copy a model or match an image in their mind. These fine-motor movements take place throughout the preschool center and may involve solitary or social play.

How Fine-Motor Skills Develop

Between the ages of three and five years, young children gain strength, coordination, and endurance in using their whole hand, as well as in using their thumb together with their index or middle finger. Handedness (the preference for left or right hand) is generally established by age four, although children still experiment with using the nondominant hand. As children's hand strength and coordination improve, they grow increasingly adept at manipulating many age-appropriate materials such as scissors, pencils, markers, crayons, blocks, puzzles, string, beads, pegs, hammers, screwdrivers, paintbrushes, the fasteners on their clothes, snap-on and screw-on

As children gain strength and coordination in using their hands, they enjoy the challenges of trying out new materials and practicing new fine-motor skills.

lids, and the switches, buttons, levers, and gears on toys and gadgets. The more proficient and confident in their fine-motor abilities preschoolers become, the more eager they are to try new materials and use them in alternative ways. Development thus spurs further growth as ability provokes interest, success encourages adventurousness, curiosity motivates practice, and practice enhances skill.

Despite these impressive advances, it is important to remember that preschoolers do not attain sophisticated levels of manual dexterity. They have physical limits; for example, they cannot make fully circular wrist motions because the cartilage in their wrists will not harden into bone until about age six (Berk, 2008). Therefore, according to Heather Tomlinson and Marilou Hyson, "writing, drawing, and cutting with precision are activities that can be difficult for many preschoolers, who are still developing comfort and agility with fine-motor work. They may experience failure and frustration if they are often expected to perform tasks requiring precise control of the hand muscles, careful perceptual judgments involving eye-hand coordination, and refined movement requiring steadiness and patience" (2009, pp. 116–117). As with all motor activities, then, young children should be encouraged to explore materials and practice skills according

Preschoolers are gaining dexterity, hand-eye coordination, strength, and flexibility as they use their hands and fingers to work with all kinds of objects and materials.

to their own expectations and internal motivation, not to meet the possibly unrealistic standards set by adults.

Teaching Strategies That Support Fine-Motor Skills

While adults should set general rather than specific expectations for preschoolers' fine-motor performance, their main goal is to encourage young children to enjoy exploring the capabilities of their hands and fingers. To support children as they develop their fine-motor skills and apply these emerging abilities to various materials and tools, adults can use the following teaching strategies.

Provide materials and activities that require the use of fingers and hands

Remember that children have different interests. Some gravitate to the art area, while others like to build with blocks, use construction tools, turn the pages of a book, do puzzles, dabble at the sand and water table, or play with cooking utensils and dress-up clothes. Note the variety of fine-motor materials these children need to carry out their intentions:

At greeting circle, Paul turns the pages of a book while Helga provides a narrative for each page. After a few minutes, they switch roles.

❖

At work time in the toy area, Ibrahim makes a row with Cuisenaire rods of increasing size, making sure they are level at the bottom.

❖

At small-group time, Celia uses a magic wand to "fish" for magnetized letters in a bowl of rice.

❖

At outside time, Joshua uses a scoop to fill a dump truck with sand. He holds a pail under the bed of the truck to catch the sand as he tips it up and empties it.

To enable preschoolers to exercise their small muscles regardless of their diverse interests, make sure there are appealing materials in each area that entail the use of children's small muscles, such as scissors (art area), thin rods (block area), magazines (book area), small figures (toy area), eggbeaters (house area), measuring spoons (sand table), and chalk (outdoor playground). Provide hard and soft materials that children can transform with their hands and fingers and that require different sets of muscles

This teacher encourages children who are at different levels in their fine-motor skills to practice writing in their own ways. One child holds the marker loosely and makes sweeping strokes, while the other child holds her marker tightly and uses controlled movements to make recognizable letters.

and varying levels of effort. This might include wooden toys they can disassemble and reassemble or batches of play dough made with different amounts of flour to vary its thickness and moldability. (For more ideas for materials that fit the interests of your group of children see the list on p. 59.)

It's also important to think about children's different interests when you plan small- and large-group times. Vary both the materials and the content of these activities so all children can be engaged using their hands and eyes to make and build, transform, investigate cause and effect, represent (write, draw, sculpt), and so on. For example, children can go on a nature walk to collect objects such as shells, stones, and twigs, and do a sorting activity with them the next day at small-group time. They are exercising fine-motor skills when they pick up objects and put them in a bag, sort them into piles, and glue them onto paper.

Think of other ways to incorporate fine-motor skills throughout the program day. Here are some examples of children using their hands and fingers in virtually every part of the daily routine:

*At **arrival time,** Penny hangs her hat on the hook in her cubby and carefully writes the first two letters of her name on the sign-in sheet next to her letter link. Then she chooses a book, sits down, and turns the pages one at a time.*

Diverse Fine-Motor Materials for Diverse Interests

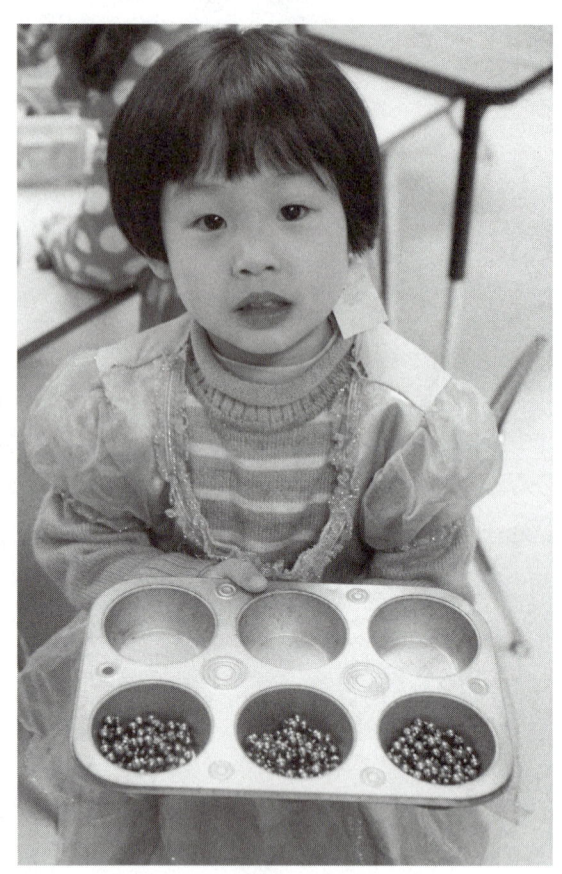

In a thoughtfully planned classroom, children with widely varying interests can find the small-motor materials they prefer to work with.

KDI 17. Fine-Motor Skills   55

Shells (left) and a variety of small manipulatives (right) are just a few examples of the many small-motor materials that can be the focus for a small-group time and/or a work-time play choice.

❖

At **message board,** Colin draws a circle with two dots and says he wants to show everyone his new glasses.

❖

At **snacktime,** Melvin writes his name on the snack chart to indicate it will be his turn tomorrow to pass out napkins.

❖

At **planning time,** Dosia says she is going to make a card for her grandma who has just left after a long visit. "I'm going to write that I love her and I miss her." When her teacher asks what materials she will use to make her card, Dosia says she will fold a piece of blue paper, and use the red crayon to write her message and draw a flower.

❖

At **work time,** Noam makes a finger painting, Alyssa sorts beads by color, Clare and Ben wrap belts around the baby dolls' clothes, and Shyroze does a five-piece jigsaw puzzle.

❖

Before **cleanup time,** Sami turns the dial on the timer to give a five-minute warning. When the time is up, Kendra flicks the lights. "I jiggled the switch," she tells her teacher.

❖

At **large-group time,** Hannah rubs two rhythm sticks together, while Lars holds the triangle in one hand and clangs the metal stick against each side in turn.

❖

At **small-group time,** Shoshona cuts red and blue construction paper into small squares, and glues the pieces in an alternating border around her picture.

❖

*At **outside time**, Devon shovels sand into a pail without spilling any of it over the sides. When the pail is full, he uses the side of the shovel to level off the top.*

❖

*Getting ready for **departure**, Rosie shows her teacher how she can fasten the Velcro strap on her boots. She demonstrates three times and comments, "My mommy says it drives her crazy!"*

Provide similar objects in a range of sizes and shapes that children can handle

Young children need to experience success — on their own terms — as they hone their fine-motor abilities. One way to guarantee feelings of accomplishment among children with emerging skill sets is to provide the same types of materials in graduated levels of difficulty. These can include the following: Duplo and Lego blocks, knob puzzles with one to three pieces, jigsaw puzzles that vary in the number and size of the pieces, pegboards with large and small holes (and pegs of corresponding widths), large and small beads for stringing, people and animal figures in different sizes, paintbrushes with thick and thin handles and different width bristles, various pencils, fat and skinny crayons and markers, and doll clothes that fasten with Velcro, buttons, ties, and zippers. Encourage children to begin with the easier materials and, as they gain skill and confidence, to move up to more challenging levels and/or use comfortable materials in new ways.

For examples of how young children develop fine-motor skills and how adults can scaffold their learning at early, middle, and later levels, see "Ideas for Scaffolding KDI 17. Fine-Motor Skills" on page 58. The ideas in the chart will help you support and gently extend children's learning as you play and interact with them during all parts of the daily routine.

At small-group time, puzzles with pieces of different sizes provide challenges for children at different levels.

Ideas for Scaffolding KDI 17. Fine-Motor Skills

Always support children at their current level and occasionally offer a gentle extension.

Earlier	Middle	Later
Children may	*Children may*	*Children may*
• Use their small muscles with some control to manipulate objects (e.g., tear paper, poke and squeeze play dough). • Do activities that require simple hand-eye coordination (e.g., put large pegs in a pegboard, stack wooden blocks, put on a hat).	• Use their small muscles with moderate control (e.g., cut with scissors, make lines and shapes with crayons). • Do activities that require moderate hand-eye coordination (e.g., string large beads, stack Duplo blocks, pour juice).	• Use their small muscles with strength, flexibility, and coordination (e.g., use scissors to cut around a heart they drew, write letterlike forms). • Use hand-eye coordination to carry out intricate activities (e.g., string small beads, build with Legos, zip a coat).
To support children's current level, adults can	*To support children's current level, adults can*	*To support children's current level, adults can*
• Provide materials that exercise children's small muscles (e.g., play dough, blocks in different sizes, sponges, squeeze bottles). • Imitate children's actions (e.g., put big pegs in the pegboard; put a hat on your head).	• Copy how children use their small muscles and describe the actions (e.g., while using the scissors, say, "I'm opening and closing my scissors just like you"). • Provide materials that require the use of hand-eye coordination (e.g., large wooden beads, plastic knives, small animal and people figures).	• Acknowledge children's abilities (e.g., "You wrote the first letter in your name"). • Ask children to demonstrate how they carried out intricate activities (e.g., "Show me how you got this part of your Lego spaceship to stick out").
To offer a gentle extension, adults can	*To offer a gentle extension, adults can*	*To offer a gentle extension, adults can*
• Label what children do with their small muscles (e.g., "You're squeezing the play dough"). • Call children's attention to what others are doing with the same materials (e.g., "Tommy put some pegs in the pegboard. He also stacked some pegs on top of each other").	• Provide materials to extend children's control of their small muscles (e.g., clay, tongs, colored pencils). • Encourage children to try one hand and then the other when they use materials.	• Pose a challenge (e.g., "I wonder what other shapes you can draw"). • Provide materials to extend children's skills (e.g., beads with smaller holes and narrower string).

Materials for Fine-Motor Movement[6]

Small building and sorting materials
- Unit blocks
- Beads and strings (large and small)
- Buttons, marbles, corks
- Shells, stones, pine cones, seed pods
- Building cubes
- Parquetry blocks
- Attribute blocks
- Nesting cups, boxes, rings
- Cuisenaire rods

Take-apart-and-put-together materials
- Washers, nuts, bolts
- Pegs and pegboards (large and small)
- Stacking rings and post
- Small Tinkertoys
- Interlocking blocks
- Interlocking shapes
- Connecting straws
- Puzzles (including ones with images of diverse people)
- Magnets
- Shape sorters and shapes
- Scales, balances
- Gear sets
- Sewing boards
- Geoboards and rubber bands
- Dowel rods with Velcro connectors
- Small nonworking appliances
- Wood scraps
- Woodworking tools and fasteners

Fasteners
- Heavy-duty staplers, staples
- Hole punch
- Paste, liquid glue, glue sticks
- Masking tape, clear tape
- Paper clips, butterfly fasteners
- Rubber bands, elastic
- Pipe cleaners, wire
- String, yarn, ribbon, shoelaces
- Needles with big eyes, thread

Pretend-play materials
- Cooking tools
- Eating utensils
- Plates, cups
- Dress-up clothes
- Dolls
- Stuffed animals
- Counting bears
- Miniature animal collections
- Little people, gnomes
- Wooden village/city/farm sets
- Puppets (animals and multiracial people)
- Wooden train sets

Games
- Simple card games, such as snap, go fish, old maid
- Memory card games
- Dominos (picture, texture)
- Picture lotto games
- Simple board games, such as Candyland

Art materials
- Variety of papers
- Paintbrushes and paint
- Markers, crayons, pencils, chalk, and other drawing tools
- Glue, tape, other fasteners
- Scissors
- Inkpads and stamps
- Jars with lids, squeeze bottles
- Modeling and molding materials: clay, play dough, etc.
- Modeling tools: rolling pins, thick dowel rods, cookie cutters, plastic knives, hamburger or tortilla press
- Collage materials
- Used stationery, greeting cards, newspapers, magazines

Reading and writing materials
- Books
- Magazines and catalogs
- Storytelling props
- Wood, plastic alphabet letter and number sets
- Writing tools and materials
- Computer equipment, typewriter

Music materials
- Simple instruments
- Recording and music-playing equipment

Fill-and-empty materials
- Sand and water
- Variety of containers, scoops, funnels
- Alternative materials for scooping and pouring: gravel, buttons, bottlecaps, rice, uncooked noodles

---

[6] Check local licensing regulations and agencies and organizations such as the Consumer Product Safety Commission (www.cpsc.gov), the American Academy of Pediatrics (www.aap.org), and the National Resource Center for Health and Safety in Child Care and Early Education (www.nrckids.org) for current information on product safety.

Socializing around fine-motor activities takes place throughout the center.

CHAPTER 5

KDI 18. Body Awareness

C. Physical Development and Health
18. Body awareness: Children know about their bodies and how to navigate them in space.

Description: Children recognize the names and locations of body parts. They are aware of their own bodies in relation to people and objects around them. Children feel, and move their bodies to, a steady beat.

At work time in the art area, Senguele draws a picture of Sue, her teacher. The figure has a face, arms, and legs. "What else do you see when you look at me?" asks Sue. Senguele adds fingers, feet, shoes, pants, and hair to her drawing.

❖

The children choose different ways to move their arms as they transition from large-group time to snacktime. "Look, Mrs. P," says Rona, "I'm making my fingers touch over my head!"

❖

At work time in the art area, Maggie paints a picture of her dad. She points out all the parts to her teacher: chest, tummy, head, pants, feet, arms, hands, fingers, and fingernails.

Body awareness in preschool involves two components. The most important is the ability to navigate the environment as children differentiate the space they occupy themselves from the space they share with other people and objects. Preschoolers explore this self-other boundary as they try out movements they increasingly but not yet fully control. Because three- and four-year-olds are still largely egocentric, they tend to think of all space as belonging to them. Gradually, however, whether through bumping into things or encountering protests from peers, they get better at establishing self-other boundaries. To develop this type of body awareness, they depend on sensory and kinesthetic feedback, that is, the perception of body movement, position, and muscular tension. The ability to move in smooth or harmonious ways (e.g., to rock to the steady beat of music or pump one's legs on a swing) is evidence of the child's emerging knowledge in this area.

The second component of body awareness is learning the names and functions of body parts. We all have a relationship with our bodies that begins to form in infancy and continues to develop well into adulthood. Preschoolers are at the stage where they are becoming increasingly aware of their bodies' different parts: e.g., *That thing sticking out of my shoulder is an arm; at the end of that is my hand; and at the end of my hand are my fingers.* Young children are intrinsically interested in their own bodies both as objects of natural curiosity and as instruments they can use to accomplish personal goals. Just as they would investigate any new material or piece of equipment, they explore the parts of their bodies and what they can use them for. Thus a child's delight is to discover: *The fingers on my hand can grasp this block. My arm is strong enough to lift and carry it to the rug.*

How Body Awareness Develops

A preschooler's body image often lags behind reality. Though growth rates vary, some children can grow as much as 6 inches and gain up to 15 pounds between the ages of three and five. A young child's idea of him- or herself can take a while to catch up to this increase in body size, and this can lead to other misjudgments, according to Heather Tomlinson and Marilou Hyson: "Learning how to monitor their bodies in space is a challenge, and frequent mishaps arise from children's lack of awareness of just how much they have grown (as when a child does not believe that a favorite shirt no longer fits) and from their lack of motor skill planning (as when a child picks the more difficult way to get somewhere)" (2009, p. 114).

Body awareness is not only tied to physical development, but also to perceptual development. We use our senses — sight, hearing, touch, taste, and smell — to monitor our body's internal states and to perceive the relationship of our bodies to our external surroundings. While preschoolers' musculatures and nervous systems are still developing, their senses and kinesthetic feedback loops — the ability to automatically adjust their movements based on sensory feedback — are already quite well developed (Tomlinson & Hyson, 2009). However, the child's ability to make intellectual sense of this sensory information is less than complete. Preschool children are still developing the cognitive strategies and language proficiency needed to interpret and communicate the incoming sensory

This boy is using feedback from all his senses to gain awareness of where his body is as he navigates along a playground divider.

data that contribute to the full awareness of and controlled use of their bodies.

There are also specific physical limitations at this age that make it important for adults to hold realistic and reasonable expectations for how young children navigate themselves through space. For example, preschoolers are farsighted and have trouble switching focus between close and distant targets (Tomlinson & Hyson, 2009). They are still developing the coordination of their binocular vision (the ability of the eyes to work together), and their limited depth perception means they tend to run into things and into each other (Pica, 2004). Their hearing is generally more developed than their vision. Thus they can easily orient their bodies in space based on the direction and volume of sounds, although distractions can temporarily disorient them. They also need to supplement their vision with tactile feedback as they judge not only their own body movements but also their proximity to people and objects around them.

As they get an overall sense of how to move their bodies in the surrounding space, preschoolers continue to be interested in the parts and functions of their bodies. Of course, this interest is also easily observed in infants and toddlers, but preschoolers show a more "scientific" interest, in that they may explore the vocabulary associated with the body's parts and seek to understand how the various parts work. They master this information through active exploration and in context, that is, while they are examining or using the parts of their body, not through rote labeling and memorization. Sometimes well-intentioned programs put a great deal of effort into explicitly teaching children basic body vocabulary (face, eyes, mouth, hands, legs, feet) rather than looking for natural openings to introduce these labels in conversation. Simply naming body parts is meaningless and arbitrary to children. They may be able to recite them, but they are just as likely to forget the labels or mix them up. By contrast, when the names are used to satisfy children's own curiosity about what things are called and what they do, this information is likelier to stick:

At greeting time, Faith rolls up her pant leg to show her teacher Becky the scrape on her leg. Becky responds by saying "Oh Faith. I see you scraped your shin."

Teaching Strategies That Support Body Awareness

To help children become aware of their bodies, navigate space with greater self-control, and learn the labels and functions of body parts, use the strategies described here. As you implement these suggestions, remember to use words that describe the orientation of the children's bodies (their position, location, direction of movement), and to label body parts and actions.

Create environments and activities that allow children to explore personal (self) space and general (shared) space

At the beginning of the program year, children need clearly marked spaces they can think of as their own. A cubby or hook marked with their name (or their symbol or letter link) tells children, "This space is mine." Large-group activities can also provide preschoolers with a space to move around in that is clearly theirs. For example, begin with movements, such as rocking or bending, where children stay in their own place. Provide visual markers, such as carpet squares or tape on the floor, to help them stay in the boundaries of their own area:

On a field trip to the beach, the children play sand angels. They lie on their backs and move their arms up and down, and their legs together

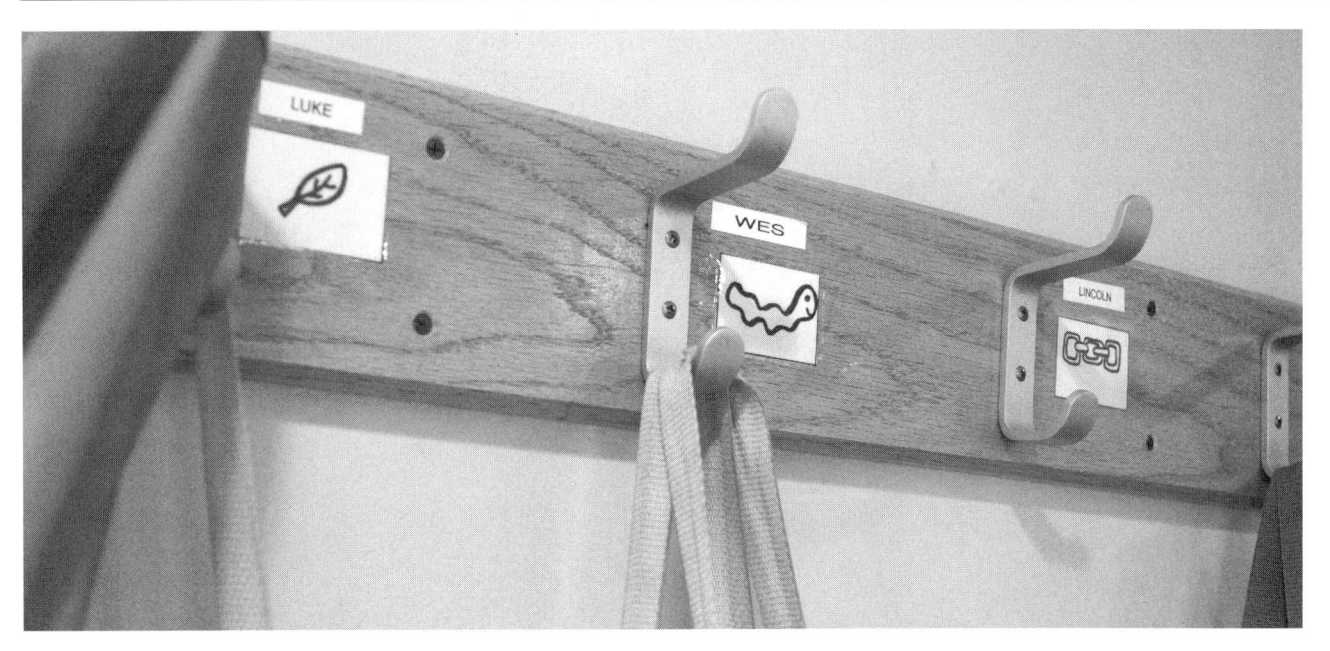

A coat hook or cubby labeled with a child's letter link or symbol helps the child learn the distinction between personal space and shared space.

and apart. They repeat these motions on their sides and stomachs. At large-group time the next day, the children sit on carpet squares and experiment with other arm and leg motions.

Once children have a sense of their own body's boundaries, encourage them to move through space shared by other people and objects. Begin with a simple locomotor movement the children have mastered (such as crawling or walking) and issue a simple challenge: "Let's see how we can move to the other side of the room without touching anyone or anything else." As the children gain more control over their bodies and their actions, vary this activity with more advanced body movements, such as galloping or skipping. Encourage children to choose their own ways to move through space, and to copy one another's movements:

At the end of greeting circle, Kyle has an idea of moving "like snakes," so all the children and their teachers lie on their stomachs and slither like snakes to their planning tables.

Working with fixed and movable objects also helps children discover self-other boundaries. For example, navigating an obstacle course helps them see where their bodies end and a piece of equipment begins. If the course contains a narrow passageway (perhaps between two cartons), they might explore whether they need to go through it alone or can squeeze through with another child. Things that children can manipulate, such as Hula-Hoops and scarves, also help them discover the relationship between themselves and objects. For example, they get a sense of where to position their bodies to catch a scarf they have thrown into the air.

Provide opportunities for children to move through different types of space in different ways

As noted earlier, children become aware of their bodies through the sensory and kinesthetic feedback they receive from the environment. Therefore, give them opportunities to move through contrasting types of spaces, including

Navigating a pathway or obstacle course provides opportunities for children to gain control of their movements as they experience the boundaries of their own bodies in relation to objects and other people.

those that are narrow and wide, low and high, straight and twisted, short and long, smooth and bumpy, and so on. Use existing spaces indoors and outside, and create others with furniture, cartons and baskets, sheet-draped tables and chairs, beanbag chairs, Hula-Hoops, tires, tape, blocks and beams, and any other safe equipment and materials.

Encourage children to move their bodies in, around, and through these spaces in different ways. For example, they might begin to move in simple ways inside the Hula-Hoop, then around the outside, then alternate movements inside and outside the hoop. Children can also experiment with the range of body movements possible when they are alone in a space versus when they share that space with others. For example, they may find that they can stretch their arms to the side when they are alone in the hoop but have to keep them at their sides if there is another child inside the hoop with them.

Give children opportunities to lead and follow during these exploratory activities. For example, ask them to suggest movements for hokey pokey, follow the leader, Simon says, or other familiar songs and games (but without winners and losers). Accept children's ideas, and repeat or clarify what they say to make it easier for others to listen, understand, and carry out their suggestions. Encourage children to observe one another and perform the same movements, but don't expect them to duplicate movements exactly. Here is an idea Stephen Sanders suggests that is suitable for older preschoolers: "In *Mirrors,* children pair off and stand facing each other. While standing in place, partners trade

Playground equipment with tight spaces to wiggle through allows children to experiment with different ways of moving through space.

off performing and imitating a series of simple movements. Variations include having one child stand in back of the performer and another in front or having one child lead a group" (2002, p. 35).

There are many other ways to encourage children to explore different body positions and movements. For example, play musical instruments at varying pitches and ask children to position their bodies according to the sound. They might stand on tiptoe for a high pitch or crouch down for a low one. At large-group times and transitions, encourage children to move their bodies in different directions or along different pathways, for example, crawling across the room forward and backward, moving in straight or zigzag patterns, or inventing ways to move up and down.

Provide opportunities for children to feel and move their bodies to a steady beat

Feeling and moving to the steady beat is an essential ability that enables children to acquire a variety of other movement skills in early childhood:

One spring day during outside time, Jessie, an adult, was pushing four-year-old Timmy on the swing. She noticed that his legs were beginning to perform the bending and straightening motion used in pumping. She began to [draw attention to] Timmy's natural movement with language, saying "BACK" as his legs went back and "OUT" as his legs went out. As Timmy felt the timing of the words, his movements became larger and more pronounced, and he moved to the steady beat. From that day on, Timmy was able to pump himself on the swing (Weikart, 2000, p. 138).

As Phyllis Weikart (2000) explains, "Steady beat is the consistent, repetitive pulse that lies within every rhyme, song, or musical selection. This pulse has even durations, occurs at equal intervals, and can be either fast or slow" (p. 122), whereas "rhythm is superimposed on the steady beat of the rhyme or song" (p. 124). A sense of steady beat must begin with a sense of steady movement, which is one reason why movement activities are so important for young children.

Infants experience steady movement while being rocked. Toddlers enjoy hearing and feeling the beat as they move their bodies to simple songs and nursery rhymes. Preschoolers also learn to maintain a steady movement as they

Hammering and swinging are steady, rhythmic motions that allow children to develop a sense of steady beat.

pound with a hammer, pump their legs on a swing, or stomp across the room like a scary monster. Using steady movement helps them develop basic timing skills, that is, an awareness of the interval between beats and the evenness of beats. Timing, in turn, may be related to children's speech fluency and later to their reading fluency (Anvari, Trainor, Woodside, & Levy, 2002; Gromko, 2005; Haraksin-Probst, Hutson-Brandhagen, & Weikart, 2008). Keeping a steady movement is thus a fundamental aspect of early learning, and moving to a steady beat is an essential activity for all preschoolers. (Moving to the overall rhythm pattern is more appropriate for second graders.)

One way that teachers can help young children make steady movements and feel a steady beat is to provide equipment with regular, predictable motions and sounds (e. g., rocking chairs and horses, swings, metronomes, and wind-up kitchen timers). A variety of activities throughout the day can provide many opportunities for preschoolers to use these materials and their bodies as they feel and express steady beat:

At large-group time, Kelly shakes her hands to the music, while Jonathan raises and lowers his arms.

❖

At work time in the construction area, Olivia steadily saws back and forth to make a groove in a block of Styrofoam.

❖

At small-group time, Jackson stamps a border of stars around his drawing. His hand goes back and forth in a steady movement between the ink pad and the paper.

❖

At outside time, Caitlin scoops sand into the pail at a steady pace while counting over and over, "One, two, three, one, two, three."

Other beat-related actions you might observe include children steadily pounding a ball of clay into a flat circle, shuffling steadily across the room to carry dirty napkins to the trash, or clapping underwater to set up a fountain of regular splashes.

Odin pounds golf tees into Styrofoam with a steady movement. "Bang, bang, bang," he says each time his hammer hits. Marta, one of his teachers, chants "Bang, bang, bang" with him. When Odin changes his chant to "Boom, boom, boom," Marta takes up the new chant.

Children can also use steady movements to mark the beat of songs, chants, and rhymes. They do this with upper body movements (e.g., using their hands to pat) and lower body movements (e.g., using their legs to march). The role of steady beat in preschool movement and music activities is discussed in the companion book *Creative Arts* (Epstein, 2012b).

Help children learn the names and functions of body parts

As noted earlier, preschoolers learn about the parts of their bodies and what they can do in the context of their exploration and play. Rote naming exercises are neither meaningful nor appropriate ways for them to learn this information. Instead, refer to children's body parts by name in ordinary conversation, for example, "Trisha, I see you're wearing a new red hat on your head" or "Lyle, can you show Ian how you kicked the ball by turning your foot to the side." When you sit down to read with a child, this is a natural time to remark on the fact that you are creating a "lap."

Build on the children's interests in exploring the things that different parts of their bodies are capable of. Imitate their movements: "I'm bending my knees too" or "Cara says we should all tap our shoulders with our thumbs." Suggest ways the children can do things with parts of their body in different positions: "Let's see how we can walk around the playground with our fingers (shoulders, knees, noses) as high in the air as we can" or "I wonder how many ways we can move with our elbows down low." As with other movement activities, encourage children to be inventive, and to observe and copy one another.

Movement activities and action songs enable children to name and move various parts of the body.

Literature and the creative arts offer many opportunities to focus on the body. Read books (*Caps for Sale* by Esphyr Slobodkina, *Emily's Balloon* by Komako Sakai), recite nursery rhymes ("One, Two Buckle My Shoe," "Jack Be Nimble"), and tell stories that feature body parts. Sing songs and chants that use body parts, such as holding up the number of fingers when singing "Ten Little Monkeys Jumping on the Bed." Children may have questions about body parts considered private, which can be discussed when reading books (such as *Body Parts* by Bev Schumaker) or during pretend play when children are dressing or undressing their "babies." Playing games is another way to help children learn about their bodies. Encourage children to name a body part to put in and take out (head, arm, foot) when they sing "Hokey Pokey." Use various noisemakers and ask children to represent the sounds with their bodies. For example, they might decide to wiggle their fingers for a jingly sound, pound their chest for a gong, and bob their head for a ticking clock. Label and describe, and encourage children to label and describe, the part(s) of the body they are using and the actions they are performing.

For examples of how preschoolers demonstrate body awareness and how adults can scaffold their learning at different developmental levels, see "Ideas for Scaffolding KDI 18. Body Awareness" on the next page. Use these ideas to supplement those already detailed as you support and gently extend children's body awareness during play and other interactions throughout the day.

Ideas for Scaffolding KDI 18. Body Awareness

Always support children at their current level and occasionally offer a gentle extension.

Earlier	Middle	Later
Children may	*Children may*	*Children may*
• Point to or name one or two body parts (e.g., head, arm, leg). • Bump into other people and things, not be aware of the relationship of their bodies to their surroundings (e.g., bump into a chair, knock over someone's blocks on their way to the water table). • Move without paying attention to or feeling a steady beat (e.g., during music, songs, or chants; while pounding play dough randomly).	• Name several body parts (e.g., knee, shoulder, neck). • Navigate around people and objects when they encounter them (e.g., stop when they get to someone's blocks and carefully step over them). • Sometimes feel a steady beat (e.g., march or pat on the beat for part of a song).	• Name many body parts (e.g., waist, shin, eyebrows). • Plan ways to navigate around people and objects beforehand (e.g., walk around the block area instead of through the middle on their way to the water table). • Maintain a steady beat (e.g., march or pat on the beat for all or most of a song).
To support children's current level, adults can	*To support children's current level, adults can*	*To support children's current level, adults can*
• Provide names for the body parts children point to. • Label children's actions when they bump into or knock over things. • Model moving to a steady beat (e.g., pound play dough rhythmically).	• Use the names of body parts in conversation (e.g., "You have paint on your cheek"). • Acknowledge when children succeed in navigating around things. • Call attention to a steady beat (e.g., tap or pat together with children on the beat; say "Tap, tap, tap" while patting to the beat of the music).	• Encourage children to name body parts in songs and chants. • Comment on how children move in space (e.g., "You went the other way so you wouldn't trip on the blocks"). • Ask children to suggest places to tap the beat during a song.
To offer a gentle extension, adults can	*To offer a gentle extension, adults can*	*To offer a gentle extension, adults can*
• Read books that feature body parts and name them for children. • Call children's attention to obstacles before they bump into them. • Pat, walk, or rock to a steady beat with children.	• Use songs and chants that feature body parts (e.g., "Hokey Pokey"). • Encourage children to think about the obstacles before they move (e.g., at planning time say "Jason already has the train tracks set up. How will you get past them to the art area?"). • Encourage children to be the leader and show the group a way to keep the steady beat.	• Provide factual books about the body. • Encourage children to think about how their actions affect how others navigate through space (e.g., "If you build your tower here, how will the other children get to the sink?"). • Ask children to start a new steady beat for others to copy.

CHAPTER 6

KDI 19. Personal Care

C. Physical Development and Health
19. Personal care: Children carry out personal care routines on their own.

Description: Children feed themselves, dress, wash their hands, brush their teeth, use tissues, and use the toilet.

At outside time, Wendy takes her snow pants off the hook and puts them on by herself, slipping the straps over her shoulders. She asks for help with her coat and hat. "When I'm older, I'll know how to zip," she says. While the teacher fastens her hat, Wendy adds, "and tie."

❖

At snack time, Bryce spills some juice on the table. He gets a paper towel to wipe it up, and throws the wet towel in the trash bin.

❖

At work time in the block area, Isaac works for a long time to undo a knot in his shoelace. "I don't need any help," he tells his teacher. When Isaac gets the lace untied, he works a while longer to make a bow. With the bow firmly in place, Isaac returns to his block play.

How Personal Care Develops

Young children enjoy taking care of themselves, and the development of their fine-motor skills (KDI 17) enables them to assume more of this responsibility. Personal care routines for preschoolers typically include getting dressed, putting on a bicycle helmet or safety goggles, using the toilet, washing their hands and face, brushing their teeth, using tissues, serving food to themselves or others, retrieving and putting away materials, and cleaning up after playing or eating. As children learn to take care of themselves, they often show interest in taking care of others too. For example, they may help or show a friend how to fasten a shoe, mop the table or floor after a classmate spills, or change the water and food in the guinea pig's bowl.

Adults are sometimes amazed at how intently children will work at mastering a self-help skill such as zipping up their jacket. The satisfaction on their faces when they succeed is obvious. It is also important to remember that we should only expect children to meet their own goal for success, not an adult's standard. (See the discussion of reasonable expectations on pp. 24–25). For example, children need not wipe every drop of a spill off the floor to be happy with the result. A child can take great pride in having brushed his or her teeth, even if the level of cleanliness doesn't meet the standards of the American Dental Association. As the National Association for the Education of Young Children (NAEYC) cautions in its guidelines for appropriate practices, "Adults are patient when there are occasional spills, accidents, and unfinished jobs" (Copple & Bredekamp, 2009, p. 164).

KDI 19. Personal Care 75

Using a trash bin that is almost as big as she is makes for a satisfying cleanup routine.

The adult works alongside the children, resisting the urge to touch up children's work until after they leave.

Of course, children also take care of their own needs in other ways. They solve problems with materials and deal with their feelings. (For these aspects of self-care, see the discussions of KDIs 4. Problem solving and 9. Emotions in the KDI companion books *Approaches to Learning* (Epstein, 2012a) and *Social and Emotional Development* (Epstein, 2012c).

Teaching Strategies That Support Personal Care

The following are some of the ways you can encourage young children to take care of their personal needs. Remember to show patience during their efforts and appreciation for their accomplishments.

Let children do things for themselves

Adults are often tempted to do things for children, such as helping them get dressed or clean up a spill, because it is faster, easier, or neater. However, young children cannot learn how to perform these actions on their own unless they are given multiple opportunities and ample time. As emphasized earlier, preschoolers are neither able nor motivated to do things perfectly. Their concern centers on mastering new skills and achieving the goals they set for themselves.

It is therefore important to resist the temptation to improve upon or correct a child's performance. Don't give the table an extra swipe with the towel or straighten the blocks on the shelf. These actions send children a message that they are not competent or "good enough," and

Labeled coat hooks (left) and cubbies (right) encourage children to be independent when getting ready to go outside or to leave for the day.

they may give up trying. If a chore involves children's health or safety, such as making sure the table is thoroughly cleaned and sanitized, staff can do it after the children leave. Remember also that children often take a long time performing personal care routines when they first learn them. For example, make sure to build enough time into the schedule for children to clean up after work time or get ready for outside time so that they can practice self-help skills without feeling rushed.

These examples show the range of things children do for themselves when self-help is encouraged and supported.

At planning time, Melton announces he is going to feed the hamster and clean out its cage. When his teacher asks what he will need, Melton replies, "The little broom and dust pan. I'll tear up newspaper for the bottom." Then he goes to the shelf where the hamster food is kept.

❖

At work time in the art area, after Becky finishes painting, she washes her brush and paint container at the sink. She undoes the Velcro strap on the smock and hangs it on the hook.

❖

After cleanup time, Nona goes to the bathroom, uses soap to wash the glue off her hands, and dries them with a paper towel. She then asks for the spray container to wash the part of the table where she was working. Then she re-rinses her hands and sits at the table for snack.

❖

At snacktime, Riana takes two apple slices and passes the basket to Peter. After she pours her own juice, she hands him the pitcher and asks, "Should I hold your cup for you?"

Serving one's own lunch from a selection of healthy foods builds dexterity and enables the child to control what and how much she eats.

❖

Before outside time, Sophie puts on her coat, zips it, and then puts on her hat and gloves by herself. "I'm all set!" she announces.

Provide children with activities and equipment for practicing the skills needed for personal care routines

Children develop competence in self-help skills not only when they carry out personal care routines but also when they perform other tasks that use comparable tools and similar physical abilities. Therefore, provide a variety of tools and activities that develop the manual dexterity children need to button a jacket, hold a pitcher steady, loop one shoelace around another, and so on. Examples of materials include beads and string, pegs and pegboards, scissors, staplers, hole punches, hammers, screwdrivers, sponges, tape, wooden spoons, brooms, and shovels.

Preschoolers also practice many self-help skills — and apply these skills to assisting others — during role play. For example, they prepare, serve, and clean up after "meals" while playing house; put clothes on dolls; or dress up as firefighters. Art and building activities also allow them to exercise many of the fine-motor abilities they use to take care of themselves as, for example, when they apply paint to paper with a toothbrush or wrap tape around a stack of blocks. Even turning the pages of a book can be a rehearsal for separating the top paper towel from the stack. The more opportunities children have to use these skills with a variety of suitable tools and materials, the more they will be able

Having real washing equipment to use with the dolls, as well as dress-up clothes with a variety of fasteners, enables children to practice personal care skills while pretending.

KDI 19. Personal Care   79

Snack Cleanup

1   2   3

Sequence charts help children follow personal care routines independently. This chart reminds children of the sequence of steps in cleaning up after snacktime: (1) Throw out your trash; (2) Put your cup in the bin; (3) Help wipe the table.

Joseph's Greeting Time

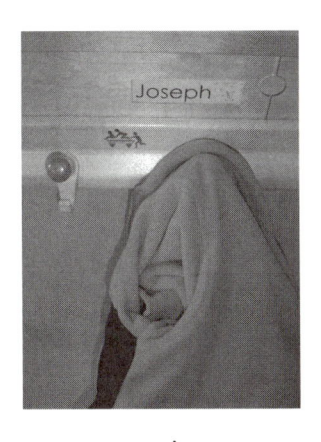

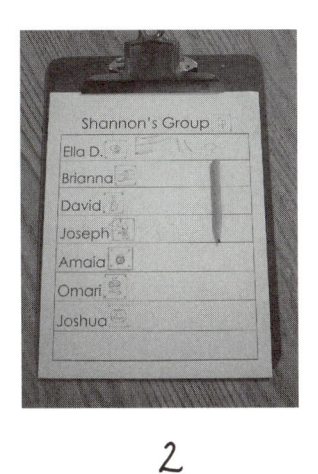

1   2   3   4

This personal sequence chart was created to help an individual child remember the steps in the morning arrival routine: (1) Hang up your coat on your coat hook; (2) Write your name (in scribbles or words) on the sign-in sheet; (3) Read and explore books with parents and a teacher in the book area; (4) Gather with classmates and adults to read the message board together.

to apply these same movements to taking care of their own physical needs. Likewise, you will find that children who practice self-help skills transfer these abilities to other activities in the classroom. For example, scrubbing a spot off the table gets them interested in scrubbing the glue off their hands. In addition to transferring specific skills, young children are simultaneously developing dispositions about the importance of taking good care of things, both the materials in the classroom and also their own bodies:

At arrival time, Alma and Monty sit on the couch and look at a book together. When Alma notices a page is ripped, she gets a piece of tape from the dispenser to fix it.

❖

At work time in the toy area, Matthew untangles the yarn looped around the handle of the Magna-Tile basket.

❖

At cleanup time in the woodworking area, Brian uses a flat-head screwdriver to pry apart two Duplo pieces.

❖

At outside time, Simone carries a bucket of water to the red tricycle and uses a large sponge to wash it. "It's sparkly clean. Now I can ride it," she tells her teacher.

For examples of how children take care of their physical needs at different stages of development and how adults can support and occasionally extend their learning, see "Ideas for Scaffolding KDI 19. Personal Care" on the next page. The suggestions in the chart, in addition to the strategies discussed earlier, will help you scaffold children's personal care skills during play and other interactions.

Children enjoy applying their developing personal care skills to assist others.

Ideas for Scaffolding KDI 19. Personal Care

Always support children at their current level and occasionally offer a gentle extension.

Earlier	Middle	Later
Children may • Require assistance in all or most personal care skills (e.g., wait for an adult to get them dressed). • Show no or little interest in doing personal care skills on their own.	*Children may* • Perform some personal care skills on their own; ask for assistance when needed (e.g., put on their coats but ask for help with their boots). • Watch and imitate other children's personal care skills.	*Children may* • Perform most personal care skills on their own (e.g., put on coats, boots, hats, and mittens with little or no assistance); work patiently to master new personal care skills. • Assist other children with personal care skills.
To support children's current level, adults can • Help children with personal care skills. • Describe the personal care need as it arises (e.g., "I'll help with your boots. Put your foot in here and push down hard. There you go!").	*To support children's current level, adults can* • Acknowledge the personal care needs children meet on their own or help others with when asked. • Be alert to signs that children are frustrated and offer help or a hint.	*To support children's current level, adults can* • Acknowledge children's personal care efforts and accomplishments (e.g., "You zipped up your coat!"). • Comment when children help one another with personal care skills.
To offer a gentle extension, adults can • Do part of a personal care skill, then encourage the child to take over (e.g., start their zipper and encourage them to pull it up the rest of the way). • Call attention to other children performing personal care skills (e.g., "I notice Stevie is putting on his hat").	*To offer a gentle extension, adults can* • Offer suggestions for how to perform personal care skills when children need assistance (e.g., "Sometimes if I wiggle my fingers, they slide in more easily"). • Refer children to one another for help (e.g., "See if Tammy can show you how she got hers to snap shut").	*To offer a gentle extension, adults can* • Pose challenges (e.g., "I wonder if there's another way to get the shirt on the doll"). • Ask children to help other children with personal care skills (e.g., "I wonder if you can show Amari how you got the soap out of the soap dispenser").

CHAPTER 7

KDI 20. Healthy Behavior

C. Physical Development and Health
20. Healthy behavior: Children engage in healthy practices.

Description: Children participate in active, physical play. They know that some foods are healthier than others. Children carry out behaviors that are healthy (e.g., cough into their elbow, wash their hands after toileting, use their own fork) and safe (e.g., wear a bike helmet, not walk in front of a moving swing, walk around a spill).

At work time in the house area, Vinnie tells his teacher, "I'm all grown up now." When she asks why he thinks that, Vinnie answers, "Because I'm eating a lot and that's why."

❖

Before snacktime, Melissa washes and dries her hands. "All clean," she says, holding them up to show Cary before sitting down. "Mine too," says Cary, spreading out his fingers on the table.

❖

At large-group time, Rowena suggests that everyone bounce from one foot to another. "I do that at my mommy's Jazzercise class," she says.

How Healthy Behavior Develops

As noted at the beginning of this book, physical activity and good nutrition are essential components of a young child's healthy development. The two are also inextricably linked, as the program manual *Healthy Young Children* (Aronson, 2002) emphasizes: "Activity has a lot to do with appetite and nutritional status. Active children need more calories than inactive ones; this means they have a better chance of getting all the required nutrients. Adequate physical exercise year-round, preferably on a daily basis, is important to a child's development because it: stimulates healthy appetites, uses calories and maintains muscle tissue, improves coordination, and encourages children to express themselves and develop social skills" (p. 55).

Helping children learn healthy eating and exercise habits is key to preventing obesity and

Using exercise bands in a movement activity is a fun way to imitate what a parent or sibling does at home and helps children begin to recognize healthy habits.

A small injury is an opportunity for the adult to model a calm and caring attitude about health emergencies as well as the skills of covering a wound.

its negative physical, emotional, social, and often academic consequences. The eating and activity patterns that lead to obesity are often established in early childhood. According to Aronson (2002), "Using food as a reward or pacifier, force-feeding, providing large portions, or requiring clean plates may contribute to obesity. Physical activity is essential to maintain a normal weight. Surprisingly, inactivity is more likely than calorie intake to result in obesity. TV watching is known to be associated with obesity, probably because of inactivity and inappropriate snacking" (p. 57).

Young children have specific exercise and nutritional needs. As described on page 6, the National Association for Sport and Physical Education (NASPE, 2009) recommends that preschoolers get at least an hour a day of intense physical activity. Early childhood programs therefore play a vital role in scheduling opportunities for vigorous exercise throughout the day. And while many nutritional requirements are met at home, children eat snacks, and sometimes meals, in their preschool classrooms or centers. In fact, snacks are an important part of a preschooler's well-balanced diet. Because their stomachs are small, young children generally can't eat enough food in three meals to meet their energy needs or satisfy their appetites. The challenge for adults is to help them eat nutritious snacks and to do so at appropriate times of the day. "Good snacks" are those that provide essential nutrients and include some protein, limited

Serving and eating nutritious snacks in a relaxed social atmosphere builds lifelong preferences for healthy eating.

Adults can model positive attitudes about trying new foods when they eat alongside children.

fat, and complex carbohydrates (such as those found in fruits, vegetables, and whole grains). Foods that are unhealthy for children (as well as grown-ups) include chips, cakes and cookies, candy, salted pretzels (unsalted are okay, preferably whole-grain), and sweetened drinks. (For a list of nutritious snacks for preschool children, see Aronson, 2002, p. 55).

Variety is another aspect of healthy nutrition. Preschoolers, like adults, need to eat food from different food groups (e.g., vegetables and grains) as well as different foods within the same group (e.g., apples and grapes). Having a variety of foods available also encourages children to try new ones, which should be introduced gradually.[7] Adults can offer different foods and the same foods prepared in different ways (for example, cooked carrots, carrot salad). Preschoolers generally enjoy eating the same foods as adults. So, if they see you enjoying something, they are more likely to want to sample it themselves. Another way to provide variety is by encouraging families to share the kinds of foods they eat at home. This allows children to experience cultural diversity in concrete ways. Even if your program does not have a great deal of diversity, you may be surprised at the variety of foods people from the same background prepare and enjoy.

In addition, providing choices and sharing control about what foods and how much of them children may eat are also essential to the development of young children's healthy eating habits. While adults determine the food that is offered, children should be able to choose whether or not to eat it. Food should never be used as a reward or punishment. The purpose of food is to satisfy hunger, not to elicit or respond to behavior. Eating to please an adult prevents children from sensing and learning to regulate their own appetites. Withholding food, especially dessert, places undue emphasis on this part of the meal and implies it is better than the other food served.

Finally, remember that other aspects of children's development affect, and are affected by, the health-related habits they develop in the early years. Many of the personal care routines described in chapter 6 (such as washing before meals, brushing one's teeth after eating, using only one's own dishes and eating

Introducing New Foods

"Food habits and the ability to eat wisely are *learned!* Children are great imitators and often mimic actions of people around them. New foods will be accepted more readily if you follow these guidelines:

- Introduce only one new food at a time.
- Serve the new food with familiar foods.
- Serve only small amounts of the new food.
- Introduce new foods only when children are hungry.
- Talk about the new food — taste, color, texture.
- Let children see you eating and enjoying the new food!
- Encourage children to taste the new food. If they reject it, accept the refusal and try again in a few weeks. As foods become more familiar, they are more readily accepted.
- Find out what is not liked about the rejected food. Often it will be accepted if prepared in a different way."

— Aronson (2002, p. 54)

---

[7] Remember, however, that a refusal or expression of dislike may reflect the fact that a preschooler's sense of taste is more acute than an adult's. Young children have additional tastebuds in the cheeks and throat, which may account for their reputation as "picky eaters" (Harris, 1986).

Children, like adults, find it easier to follow safety practices that are an everyday part of their social world.

utensils, putting on a bike helmet) are also part of healthy behavior. For example, brushing one's teeth removes sugar from the enamel and establishes a healthy self-care habit. Moreover, there are many social aspects to healthy behavior, such as eating with others and enjoying the conversation surrounding a meal. A pleasant and relaxed eating environment helps young children develop healthy and positive attitudes about food. Likewise, when physical activity is for the fun of it, without competition or performance pressure, exercise is something to look forward to rather than a chore or expectation imposed from the outside.

In sum, children, like adults, find it easier to act "well" when they receive support from others. Exercising and eating nutritious foods are facilitated by the social and emotional context in which they occur. When the whole class — adults and children together — engage in healthy behavior, children come to assume that this is simply how living is done:

At work time in the house area, Bret looks at Kimi and says, "How did you get so tall? What did you eat?" Kimi says her mom cooked broccoli the night before. When Bret asks what that is, Kimi replies, "It's like a little tree." "I like apples," says Bret. "They come from a tree too."

Teaching Strategies That Support Healthy Behavior

To promote healthy behavior in young children — including habits related to eating, exercise, and hygiene — adults can use the teaching strategies suggested below.

Model healthy behavior yourself

"The habits children learn during their preschool years will significantly affect their future health" (Aronson, 2002, p. 61). This is true of exercise patterns, dietary habits, and hygiene routines. The primary source of this early learning is the significant adults who young children seek to emulate. Therefore, the more you engage in healthy behaviors as a regular part of your daily routine, the more preschoolers are apt to adopt these behaviors themselves.

In addition to the behavior itself, remember that you are modeling an attitude toward that behavior. If you express displeasure, squeamishness, or resentful compliance, children will pick up on these negative sentiments and internalize them as well. If, on the other hand, you express pleasure in exercising your body, sensory delight in sampling different foods, and satisfaction in practicing good hygiene, children will develop these positive attitudes instead:

For their summer potluck, the families at one child care center bring their favorite dishes that feature fruit, including orange and raisin salad, chicken with cherries and shredded coconut, apple-pecan muffins, and blueberry cobbler. "I'm going to try some of everything," the teacher announces. As she samples each food, she asks the parents about the ingredients and how the dish was prepared. The children decide they want to make the orange-raisin salad for snacktime. "We could put in cherries and apples too," they suggest.

Provide opportunities for children to engage in healthy behavior

As described in previous chapters, opportunities for exercise, healthy eating, and good hygiene should abound throughout the program day. Children get exercise when they move their bodies in a variety of nonlocomotor ways (e.g., bending, twisting, swinging, and rocking), explore locomotor actions (walking, climbing, running, hopping, skipping, marching, and galloping), and move with objects (including things to move with, move on, and make move). They learn about good hygiene when they practice personal care routines such as washing before and after meals, using their own utensils, putting on bicycle helmets, wiping their nose with a tissue, and brushing their teeth. Their inherent interest and pride in mastering these self-help skills is a natural motivator for them to develop healthy habits. The more you give children the

A hands-on field trip to a pizza shop lets children know there is a make-it-yourself alternative to purchased pizza.

90   *Physical Development and Health*

On a field trip to an apple orchard, teachers, children, and family members enjoy outdoor exercise and learn more about the origins of a healthy food. Back in the classroom, children explore apples and make a chart of their characteristics.

time, opportunity, and materials to practice and refine these skills, the more they will become embedded as daily habits.

Learning about food and nutrition can also be easily integrated into the daily routine. Children can plan, prepare, serve, and eat simple and nutritious snacks. Curriculum writer Laura Colker (2005) says many teachers shy away from cooking with children because they worry about the potential for accidents, transmission of germs, or other hazards. However, there are many simple steps you can take to protect children's safety: For example, use dull knives, heavy potholders, and warm rather than hot water. To minimize health risks, wash ingredients thoroughly, keep foods at the recommended temperature to prevent bacterial growth, and discourage nibbling during cooking. Preschoolers generally have enough self-control and understanding of time that they can wait to eat if you keep the preceding activity short and explain that everyone will eat when it's over. It also helps to provide a concrete measure, such as a timer, for children to watch. (For other specific safety and health suggestions, as well as ideas on how and what to cook with young children, see Colker, 2005.)

During meals and snacktime, preschoolers can identify and discuss the properties of the foods they are eating. Engage them in observing and describing the appearance, sound, smell, feel, and taste of different fruits, vegetables, and other healthy foods. At small-group time, plan an activity in which the children guess a food from one attribute (e.g., closing their eyes and experiencing just its smell or taste) and then open their eyes to verify their guess. Here is an example of an activity in which children investigate a common food with all their senses:

At small-group time, the teacher gives each child a quarter of a small cantaloupe along with a metal spoon, plastic knife, and large paper plate. The children explore scooping out the seeds, separating the pulp from the peel, and comparing the texture and moisture of the fruit and the rind. They smell it, taste it, and describe what the melon feels like on their tongue. One child observes that the cantaloupe is "sweet" like watermelon, but "lots mushier."

Other activity ideas include taking a class field trip to a farm to see where and how "real" food is grown or visiting a farmers' market or food coop to explore places, other than the supermarket, where food is sold (Aronson, 2002).

For examples of how young children develop healthy behavior at different stages of development and how adults can support and gently extend their learning, see "Ideas for Scaffolding KDI 20. Healthy Behavior" on the next page. The chart provides additional ideas for scaffolding healthy behavior during your play and interactions with the young children in your program. Following this is a summary of all the physical development and health strategies in this book.

Ideas for Scaffolding KDI 20. Healthy Behavior

Always support children at their current level and occasionally offer a gentle extension.

Earlier	Middle	Later
Children may	*Children may*	*Children may*
• Be reluctant to join in physical activity (e.g., they prefer to be pulled in a wagon or to sit and watch other children play). • Be unaware of the nutritional value of food. • Be unaware of healthy behaviors (e.g., return to play after using the bathroom without washing their hands; put toys in their mouths).	• Be physically active (e.g., run, climb, ride a tricycle). • Know that food is important to help them grow up to be strong and healthy (e.g., "If I drink milk my teeth will get white and strong"). • Carry out healthy behaviors or do some of the steps in them (e.g., cough in their elbow; wipe their nose with a tissue but not throw it in the trash).	• Engage in sustained physical activity; know their exertions are good for their bodies (e.g., "I'm climbing to the top. My muscles are getting strong!"). • Know that some foods are healthier than others (e.g., "My mommy doesn't buy junk for dessert any more, only fruit"). • Carry out all the steps in healthy behaviors (e.g., wash their hands and use the paper towel to turn off the faucet).
To support children's current level, adults can	*To support children's current level, adults can*	*To support children's current level, adults can*
• Call attention to other children's physical activities. • Serve children healthy food but never force them to eat anything. • Stop unhealthy behaviors (e.g., remind children to wash their hands or that toys stay in their hands, not in their mouths).	• Join in children's physical activities. • Acknowledge children's statements about which foods are good for their bodies (e.g., "Yes, milk does make your teeth strong"). • Acknowledge children's healthy behaviors (e.g., "You remembered to cough in your elbow").	• Confirm that physical activity and healthy bodies go together. • Discuss with children which foods are healthier than others. • Acknowledge when children do all the steps of a healthy behavior.
To offer a gentle extension, adults can	*To offer a gentle extension, adults can*	*To offer a gentle extension, adults can*
• Encourage children to join in physical activities. • Comment that a food is healthy (e.g., "Carrots are good for our bodies"). • Model and label healthy behavior (e.g., "I blew my nose. Now I have to throw away the tissue and wash my hands").	• Comment on the link between physical activity and having a healthy body (e.g., "You ran a lot today. Your legs are getting stronger"). • Share how other foods are good for the body (e.g., "Carrots help our eyes see better"). • Provide visual reminders of multi-step healthy behaviors (e.g., a chart at the sink with photos of each step of hand washing).	• Explain other ways that children's physical activity benefits their body (e.g., "Running up the hill makes your legs stronger and is also good for your heart"). • Converse with children about the healthy foods they and the adults like (e.g., "Jessa likes blueberries and I like snap peas. What healthy foods do you like?"). • Connect children's behaviors to healthy practices (e.g., "You coughed in your elbow to keep from spreading germs").

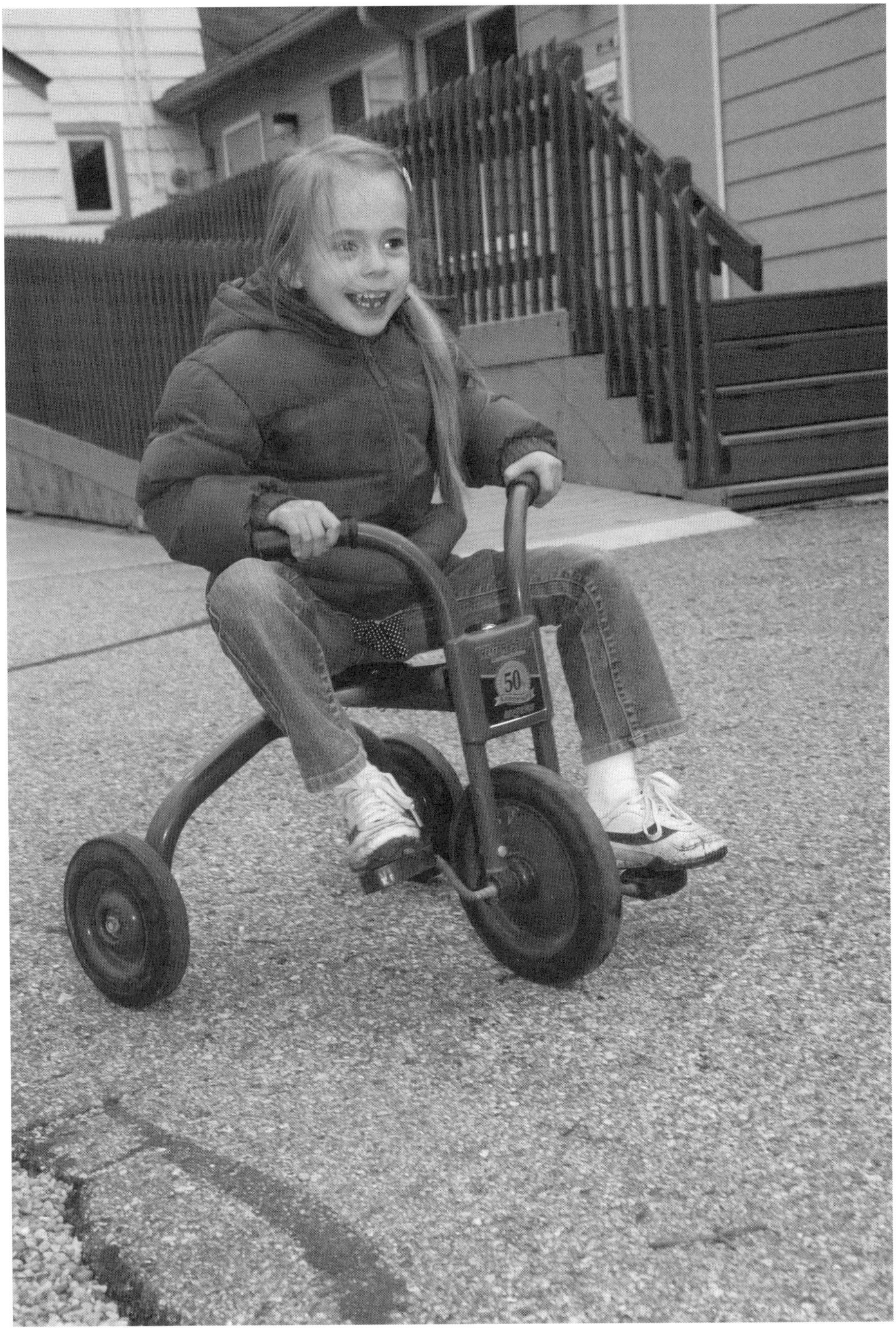

Physical Development and Health Strategies: A Summary

General teaching strategies that support physical development and health

- Provide space for children to explore and practice motor skills.
- Provide children with equipment and materials for exploring and practicing motor and self-help skills.
- Provide time for children to explore and practice motor and self-help skills throughout the day.
- Model and guide emerging physical skills and healthy behaviors.
- Add language to describe behavior related to physical development and health.

Teaching strategies that support gross-motor skills

- Encourage children to explore a wide range of positions and movements.
- Encourage children to build movement skills in sequence.
- Provide interesting materials to accompany children's movements.
- Provide children with experiences and materials for exploring movement concepts.

Teaching strategies that support fine-motor skills

- Provide materials and activities that require the use of fingers and hands.
- Provide similar objects in a range of sizes and shapes that children can handle.

Teaching strategies that support body awareness

- Create environments and activities that allow children to explore personal (self) space and general (shared) space.
- Provide opportunities for children to move through different types of space in different ways.
- Provide opportunities for children to feel and move their bodies to a steady beat.
- Help children learn the names and functions of body parts.

Teaching strategies that support personal care

- Let children do things for themselves.
- Provide children with activities and equipment for practicing the skills needed for personal care routines.

Teaching strategies that support healthy behavior

- Model healthy behavior yourself.
- Provide opportunities for children to engage in healthy behavior.

References

American Academy of Pediatrics, Committee on Public Education. (2001). Children, adolescents, and television [Position statement]. *Pediatrics, 107*(2), 423–426. doi:10.1542/peds.107.2.423

Anvari, S. H., Trainor, L. J., Woodside, J., & Levy, B. A. (2002). Relation among musical skills, phonological processing and early reading ability in preschool children. *Journal of Experimental Psychology, 83,* 111–130. doi:10.1016/S0022-0965(02)00124-8

Aronson, S. S. (Ed.). (2002). *Healthy young children: A manual for programs* (4th ed.). Washington, DC: National Association for the Education of Young Children.

Berk, L. E. (2008). *Infants and children: Prenatal through middle childhood* (6th ed.). Boston, MA: Pearson/Allyn & Bacon.

Colker, L. J. (2005). *The cooking book: Fostering young children's learning and delight.* Washington, DC: National Association for the Education of Young Children.

Copple, C., & Bredekamp, S. (Eds.). (2009). *Developmentally appropriate practice in early childhood programs serving children from birth through age 8* (3rd ed.). Washington, DC: National Association for the Education of Young Children.

Epstein, A. S. (2007). *The intentional teacher: Choosing the best strategies for young children's learning.* Washington, DC: National Association for the Education of Young Children.

Epstein, A. S. (2012a). *Approaches to learning.* Ypsilanti, MI: HighScope Press.

Epstein, A. S. (2012b). *Creative arts.* Ypsilanti, MI: HighScope Press.

Epstein, A. S. (2012c). *Social and emotional development.* Ypsilanti, MI: HighScope Press.

Gallahue, D. L. (1995). Transforming physical education curriculum. In S. Bredekamp & T. Rosegrant (Eds.), *Reaching potentials: Transforming early childhood curriculum and assessment* (Vol. 2, pp. 125–144). Washington, DC: National Association for the Education of Young Children.

Gallahue, D. L., & Donnelly, F. C. (2003). *Developmental physical education for all children* (4th ed.). Champaign, IL: Human Kinetics.

Graham, G., Holt/Hale, S., & Parker, M. (2004). *Children moving: A reflective approach to teaching physical education.* St. Louis, MO: McGraw-Hill.

Gromko, J. E. (2005). The effect of music instruction on phonemic awareness in beginning readers. *Journal of Research in Music Education, 53*(3), 199–209. doi:10.2307/3598679

Haraksin-Probst, L., Hutson-Brandhagen, J., & Weikart, P. S. (2008). *Making connections: Movement, music, and literacy.* Ypsilanti, MI: HighScope Press.

Harris, A. C. (1986). *Child development.* St. Paul, MN: West Publishing.

Jensen, E. (2000). Moving with the brain in mind. *Educational Leadership, 58*(3), 34–37.

Kagan, S. L., Moore, E., & Bredekamp, S. (Eds.). (1995, June). *Reconsidering children's early development and learning: Toward common views and vocabulary.* Goal 1 Technical Planning Group Report 95-03. Washington, DC: National Education Goals Panel.

Manross, M. A. (2000). Learning to throw in physical education class: Part 3. *Teaching Elementary Physical Education, 11*(3), 26–29.

National Association for Sport and Physical Education. (2009). *Active start: A statement of physical activity guidelines for children from birth to five years* (2nd ed.). Reston, VA: Author.

National Center for Health Statistics. (2004). *Health, United States, 2004.* Hyattsville, MD: Author.

Nebraska Department of Education. (2005, June). *Nebraska early learning guidelines: A resource to support young children's development and learning.* Retrieved from http://www.nde.state.ne.us/ech/ELGuidelines/ELG_3to5.pdf

Pica, R. (1997). Beyond physical development: Why young children need to move. *Young Children, 52*(6), 4–11.

Pica, R. (2004). *Experiences in movement: Birth to age 8.* Clifton Park, NY: Delmar Learning.

Sanders, S. W. (2002). *Active for life: Developmentally appropriate movement programs for young children.* Washington, DC: National Association for the Education of Young Children.

Sawyers, K. S. (with Colley, E., & Icaza, L.). (2010). *Moving with purpose: 54 activities for learning, fitness, and fun.* Ypsilanti, MI: HighScope Press.

Stellaccio, C. K., & McCarthy, M. (1999). Research in early childhood music and movement education. In C. Seefeldt (Ed.), *The early childhood curriculum: Current findings in theory and practice* (3rd ed., pp. 179–200). New York, NY: Teachers College Press.

Strubank, R. (1991). Music and movement throughout the daily routine. In N. A. Brickman & L. S. Taylor (Eds.), *Supporting young learners* (Vol. 1, pp. 104–111). Ypsilanti, MI: HighScope Press.*

Tomlinson, H. B., & Hyson, M. (2009). Developmentally appropriate practice in the preschool years — ages 3–5: An overview. In C. Copple & S. Bredekamp (Eds.), *Developmentally appropriate practice in early childhood programs serving children from birth through age 8* (3rd ed., pp. 111–148). Washington, DC: National Association for the Education of Young Children.

Weikart, P. S. (2000). *Round the circle: Key experiences in movement for young children*. Ypsilanti, MI: HighScope Press.

White House Task Force on Childhood Obesity. (2010). *Solving the problem of childhood obesity within a generation: Report to the President*. Washington, DC: Author. Retrieved from http://www.letsmove.gov/sites/letsmove.gov/files/TaskForce_on_Childhood_Obesity_May2010_FullReport.pdf

Wood, C. (2007). *Yardsticks: Children in the classroom, ages 4–14* (3rd ed.). Turner Falls, MA: Northeast Foundation for Children.

---

*Also available at the HighScope *Extensions* archive at highscope.org.